ELIJAH MAN ON FIRE

Bill Gehm

The Grace Collective Publishing

Cover design includes elements from Freepik.

Contents

PROLOGUE 2

1. DEBUT 7

2. DEVELOPMENT - SANCTIFICATION 19

3. DESTINY 41

4. DEPRESSION 81

5. DETERMINATION 115

6. DEPARTURE 150

7. DYNAMICS 168

8. DIRECTIVE 187

9. DAY OF THE LORD 197

This book is the fruit of much more than my own labor; it is the result of faithful friends and family who gave of themselves with generosity and love.

I am deeply grateful to my dear friends, Ric and Kathie Vogelgesang, Shane and Lauren Warden, and Eric and Chris Smith for their extra effort this past year. Your encouragement and support have meant more than words can express.

To my niece, Mary Venable, thank you for your patience and diligence in editing and re-editing this manuscript time and again. Your careful attention and commitment helped shape this work into what it is today.

Most of all, I offer a special and heartfelt thanks to my dear friend and sister, Angela Gray.

Angela, none of this would be possible without your sacrifice and tireless effort. You took my sermons and faithfully transcribed them into this wonderful book. Your insight and unique ability to communicate my heart are truly priceless. I thank God for our special friendship and for the burden He placed on your heart to help bring this book to life.

May the Lord bless each of you richly.

PROLOGUE

"Forever, O LORD, your word is settled in heaven. Your faithfulness endures to all generations; You established the earth, and it abides. They continue this day according to Your ordinances, for all are Your servants." (Psalm 119:89-91)

Every summer, my wife and I travel across our nation, visiting our loved ones scattered from one side to the other. Our nation is in trouble. Tragic headlines are so common that they have become the background beat of our lives. Whether we open our internet browser, turn on our televisions, or dial into our favorite radio stations, we see and hear the same things: war, mass shootings, political upheaval, riots, and the like. In addition to national and global unrest, we are plagued by our own cares, but I am not afraid.

I have enjoyed many hobbies throughout my life, but for the past several years, my favorite hobby, perhaps my only hobby, is reading the Word of God. I have the greatest job in the world. My church pays me to study and preach the Bible. I have experienced highs and lows just like anyone else, but I still love my job. I love it more today than when I preached my first sermon because the Bible is not an ancient book.

It is an eternal book, as relevant and life-giving as the God from whom it flows. I had no idea how strongly His Word could cling or how deeply His Word could anchor, but after fifty years, I have seen God prove Himself faithful and His Word to be true, not only in my own life, but also in the lives of those I have pastored.

This is why I am not afraid. I am concerned, but I am not afraid. No matter how bad it seems, we know how it ends. It ends with a wedding, a feast. Jesus is coming back. We are privy to inside information. The Bible is like a time machine that allows us to look to the past, the present, and the future. In all of it, we find the presence of the Lord Jesus. We find that the will of God prevails, and God's Word always comes true.

I often reflect on my life and the many situations I found myself in, and I have thought, "If I knew then what I know now, I would have handled that season differently." God saved me when I was sixteen years old. I flipped my motorcycle end over end down a hill. I should have died, but God spared me. Jesus met me at the bottom of the hill. He invited me to follow Him, and I said yes.

It was the defining moment that changed everything. I drew a line in the dirt that day, and I have never looked back, but I did not understand the impact of my decision. I was a sixteen-year-old boy from Denver, Colorado, yet somehow my humble life took on eternal significance in the hands of God. Under the Lordship of Jesus Christ, He has done more in and with my life than I even thought to imagine. I did not know I would pastor a church in Amarillo, Texas. I did not know I would be part of a worldwide radio and internet ministry.

I do not know what will happen with the remainder of my time here on earth. I do know I am a living example of His saving grace. I am His light in the darkest corners of my world. I love the people around me and carry His hope into their bleakest situations. I represent the Lord, and my God is still the God who saves.

I serve the same God that Elijah served. I am on the same side. Some of the people in the Bible have become my friends, and Elijah is one of my best friends. I feel like I know him personally. He profoundly influenced my life and ministry, not just because he stood atop a mountain and called down fire, but because he hid away in fear inside a cave. Scripture says, "Elijah was a man with a nature like ours." (James 5:17)

Elijah was human, and Bill Gehm is human. There have been seasons when my faith has held strong and barely wavered. There have been seasons when fear and doubt plagued my mind and heart, but I still walked on. There have been seasons when fear, doubt, anger, and disappointment overtook me, and I did sit down, but God was faithful and gracious. He picked me up, strengthened my mind, body, and soul, took my hand, and said, "Let's keep walking."

The good news is that this is not Elijah's story. It is not Bill Gehm's story. This book is about the Lord. It is about how the Lord takes ordinary people and invites them to participate in His extraordinary plan. It is about how the Lord is the source and uses us to be His vessels, as flawed as we may be. It is about how the Lord continually works in us until we look more and more like His Son. It is about the Lord completing the work He started. We can study, dissect, analyze, and interpret Elijah's words and deeds in the tiniest detail, but his life and ministry boil down to one simple message: "The LORD God of Israel lives" (1 Kings 17:1).

Elijah could never have imagined his life's impact, not only on the present generation of believers he lived in but also on the generations of believers to come hundreds of years after he was gone. All he knew was that Israel was in trouble. They were headed in the wrong direction, and he knew he needed to do something.

We need to do something. I know we all want to do something, but what? We move from one day to the next with the simple goal of surviving. With the world's weight on our shoulders, we often look down. If we peer too far ahead, we become overwhelmed. If we look within, we grow discouraged.

We must follow Elijah's example. We simply say, "Here I am, Lord. Send me." Then we go! We represent the Lord Jesus, and I am here to remind us of His words:

"Look up and lift your heads, because your redemption draws near." (Luke 21:28). Those are not my words. Those are the words of the Lord Jesus. It is His promise, and Jesus is the foundation of our faith, salvation, hope, and future. It is firm and settled in the heavens. Salvation is here!

"But I saw no temple in it, for the Lord God Almighty and the Lamb are its temple. The city did not need the sun or the moon to shine in it, for the glory of God illuminated it. The Lamb is its light. And the nations of those who are saved shall walk in its light, and the kings of the earth bring their glory and honor into it. Its gates shall not be shut by day (there shall be no night there). And they shall bring the nations' glory and honor into it. But there shall by no means enter anything that defiles, or causes an abomination or a lie, but only those written in the Lamb's Book of Life." (Revelation 21:22-28)

Chapter One

DEBUT

IT HAS TO START SOMEWHERE

ISRAEL HAS A SIN PROBLEM

God never wanted His people to blend in. Everything about Israel's existence, from its conception in the barren womb of an elderly woman named Sarah to its spectacular deliverance from bondage in Egypt, shows that God chose to make Himself known to the nations through His chosen people. He wanted to be their God, and He wanted them to be His people, separate and distinct from the rest of the surrounding nations.

What an honor to be chosen by Almighty God for such a purpose. God intended for Israel's reach to be far more significant than that of a great nation of its day. He intended for their legacy to be eternal and everlasting in the person of Jesus Christ. God wanted to protect them. He wanted to preserve Israel to reveal Himself to the rest of the world.

But Israel rejected God as their ruler, and they wanted a king, just like every other nation. God told the prophet Samuel, "They have rejected Me." (1 Samuel 8:7)

After King Solomon died, Israel split into two kingdoms: Judah, made up of the tribes of Judah and Benjamin, and Israel, made up of the ten remaining tribes. Every king after Solomon was more wicked than their predecessor, until we come to Ahab.

Ahab was married to one of the most wicked women in Israel's history, Jezebel. I call her "Jezzy". She worshiped the false god, Baal. In fact, her name means, "Baal is my husband." She fully devoted herself to this idol and led her husband and the rest of Israel to do the same. The king and his wife slaughtered the prophets of Jehovah and built altars to Baal.

Israel was in total darkness. Its sin problem seemed hopeless, but God's plan for Israel had not changed. He was ready to expose Baal. Baal was not God. He was a fake. He was ready to remind Israel of who their God truly was, is, and forever will be. All he needed was someone to say, "Here I am! Send me," and Elijah said, "I will be that man."

Elijah busted into the king's courts and dropped the challenge. "As the LORD God of Israel lives, before whom I stand, there shall not be dew nor rain these years, except at my word." (1 Kings 17:1) Who was Elijah?

ELIJAH PRAYED EARNESTLY

"Elijah was a man with a nature like ours, and he prayed earnestly that it would not rain; and it did not rain on the land for three years and six months. And he prayed again, and the heavens gave rain, and the earth produced its fruit." (James 5:17-18)

James tagged Elijah as a man like us with one distinguishing characteristic: he prayed earnestly. Did he start praying before he confronted Ahab? We don't know, but history shows us that mighty works of God often begin with a burden given to a man or woman of God in prayer.

Baal was the "sky god." His worshipers believed he could control the weather, including the rain. Baal was no god at all. Elijah knew the One who could shut up the heavens. Elijah knew that Jehovah was God. Elijah watched Israel's descent into spiritual decay and chaos, and he took upon himself the burden of reminding them of the truth with the hope of restoring Jehovah's rightful place as God of Israel. God wanted Israel to come back.

The world is headed for destruction. Even unbelievers can sense there is something wrong. The Good News is that God is not looking to destroy people. God wants to save people, and He wants us to be part of that rescue mission. If we underestimate the importance of prayer in accomplishing that goal, may I remind us of our Savior, Jesus Christ?

God called upon Jesus to bear a burden no one else could carry, and the weight of the cross followed Jesus everywhere as He carried out His earthly ministry. In prayer, Jesus knew the importance of constant communion with His Father for strength and encouragement. At one point, even Jesus confessed that He was overwhelmed and sorrowed by the task that awaited Him. When the appointed moment arrived for Him to carry out His mission on the cross, He dared not face it without first spending time on His knees before His Father.

My greatest works did not begin at a pulpit. My greatest works began with a burden given to me by the Lord during my moments of prayer. In 1980, I answered the call of God. "*Amarillo by morning.*" I was hired to be the (church's) youth pastor of a church that was falling apart. I cannot overstate how messed up this church was, and I begged God to release me and let me and my family return to our beloved home in the Rocky Mountains of Colorado. God said "No!" So I continued to pray.

I knew that was the only way I could endure. In those times of prayer, God placed in my heart a burden to start a new, living work out of this dying work, and the seeds of Grace Church were planted.

Several years later, at what seemed like the pinnacle of our success as a church, God gave me a new burden for the intersection of Western and Plains in my city, leading me to purchase an old grocery store that would eventually become the new location of Grace Church. What most did not know at that time was that prior to that moment, I had spent countless hours on my face before God because I knew my church was becoming too comfortable with the status quo. We all looked alike, talked alike, and had the same backgrounds, but I knew God called us to reach a city growing more diverse every year. I was tired of being nice. God answered my prayer: "We're moving, and it won't be nice!"

God did not call me to live a nice, comfortable life. He called me to seek and save the lost in Amarillo, Texas. We can become overwhelmed at the scope of the needs around us, and if we do not remain connected to the Source of our faith, fear will paralyze us. Where do we start?

May I suggest we follow Elijah's lead? Better yet, how about we follow Jesus's example? We pray earnestly. We can never be more in public for God than we are in private with God, and the posture of faith often begins by dropping to our knees, sometimes even on our faces, before God in prayer. Ask God for a burden, an assignment, and the strength and persistence to see it through. Nothing is within our control except obedience and faithfulness to the Lord.

Few will be called to confront the king, and most will not be given a pulpit. All of us are called to represent the Lord Jesus using the Spiritual Gift He gave us. Prayer connects us to the only living God, provides direction and clarity, and empowers us as we use our gifts.

God's sovereignty placed Elijah in Israel at the right time and in the right place, and Elijah prayed because he believed that God could save Israel. Prayer placed him in the prime position to be called upon to help fulfill that mission, and Elijah did not let go.

Look around. Ask God for a burden for a single person, a family, or your neighborhood. God places us in different parts of the world so we can light up the darkness with the truth of the Gospel. Pray earnestly, and do not underestimate the work of prayer. Elijah's prayers shut up the heavens. They called down fire. They brought the rain. Those were great miracles. We pray for God to save people. We can change the life of one person, entire families, or maybe even our own cities, if we take up the burden and pray fervently for them. Our God is still the God who saves.

Elijah, men and women, pray.

ELIJAH HAD THE RIGHT NAME

God did give Israel a good king, not a perfect king, but a Godly king in the man David, who did his best to honor the name of the Lord. But by the time we get to Ahab and Jezzy, Jehovah's name is not only forgotten, but this evil duo actively sought to erase His name from Israel altogether by killing His prophets. But once again, God had a man and put a fire in his heart for the name and Word of God.

Who was Elijah? Where did he come from? The Bible reveals very little about Elijah's origin story. We know he was from

Tishbe. All we really know about Tishbe is that it was a town in Gilead. It did not seem to be a significant town. We never met his parents. He does not seem to be from an influential Jewish lineage, which I find interesting because he was such a powerful and influential voice in Israel's history. Basically, Elijah was a nobody from nowhere, a whosoever from wherever, but Elijah had the right name. Elijah's name means "*My God is Jehovah.*" Elijah knew Jehovah was his God.

"As the LORD God of Israel lives, before whom I stand." (1 Kings 17:1)

Elijah's boldness did not come from his confidence in himself. It came from his confidence in his God. His background, credentials, breeding, and pedigree no longer mattered because once he made Jehovah his God and His will his mission, all that mattered was that Elijah's God was the true and living God. God empowered him with His Name, Word, and Spirit, giving Elijah the strength he needed to stand in the courts of Ahab.

We cannot convince anyone of the truth of the Gospel of Jesus Christ until we have made Jesus the Savior and Lord of our own lives. But when we receive that revelation of who Jesus is and say "yes" to Him, we are on a mission to make His name known worldwide. His name is the only name that allows us access to God. His name is the only name by which we receive salvation. I was a sixteen-year-old kid from Colorado, a nobody from nowhere, but God told me to "go." So, I went. Not because I had great influence, wisdom, or wealth, but because I had the same power behind me that Elijah had when he went before the king. I had the name of Jesus. I had His Word. I had the Holy Spirit. Jehovah was my God. Jesus was my Savior and my Lord. I had the right name. Elijah men and women have the right name, which gives us the boldness to stand strong and not shrink back, even in the face of our fiercest enemy!

ELIJAH KNEW HIS ENEMY

"As the LORD God of Israel lives, before whom I stand, there shall not be dew nor rain these years, except at my word." (1 Kings 17:1)

Elijah knew his fight was not with people. Elijah placed the target squarely on the forehead of the imaginary god, Baal. Worshipers believed Baal to be the sky god, the one who controlled the rain, and an ally of the sun god. By challenging Baal's supposed power and authority, Elijah sought to remove any question as to who Israel's true God was. Their God was Jehovah, and He was more than just *a god*. He was *the God* above all others.

Long before he called down fire on Mount Carmel, the fire of God ignited in Elijah's heart somewhere along the way. A veil of darkness had fallen over God's people. Ahab should have recognized his position as king and led his people to the light, but he was as blind as the rest. He followed the voice of his wicked wife, who sought to remove the Name and the Word of God from God's people. This was a dangerous plan because God's Name and His Word were the only strength the nation of Israel possessed.

Elijah did not seek to destroy Ahab or the people of Israel. Elijah sought to destroy the works of darkness. If there had been no rain in Israel until Elijah had called for it, he would have exposed Baal as a phony. God would prevail. Israel's history was filled with God's triumph over His enemies. God's sovereignty would be maintained regardless of Israel's faithfulness or obedience, but Elijah recognized that if Israel continued in its rebellion against God, it would bring about their own destruction. Elijah stood up for the truth. He did not stand against the people. He stood up for the Lord, as the God of Israel lives. God was not dead. He was alive, and God did not come to destroy Israel. He sent a man of God with the fire of the Holy Spirit.

"For we do not wrestle against flesh and blood, but against principalities, against powers, against the rulers of the darkness of this age, against spiritual hosts of wickedness in the heavenly places." (Ephesians 6:12)

The enemy always seeks to destroy people. His tactics have not changed, but neither has our God. The apostle Paul said, "For the weapons of our warfare are not carnal but mighty in God for pulling down strongholds." (2 Corinthians 10:4)

God did not send Jesus into the world to condemn it, but to save it. The Lord Jesus already won 2000 years ago when He crushed the head of the snake. His objective is to save souls. Those of us who have received salvation are on the winning side. We proclaim the truth. Our God saves. Jesus Christ died for our sins and rose from the grave. Jesus Christ is the only way to salvation. Jesus Christ is coming back, and those who do not receive Him are headed for destruction. But there is good news! Jesus did not come to destroy, but to seek and save! Elijah, men and women know with whom the fight lies.

ELIJAH KNEW HIS CALLING

"Watch, stand fast in the faith, be brave, be strong. Let all that you do be done with love." (1 Corinthians 16:13-14) It is plausible that Israel forgot who their God really was because the truth was buried deeper and deeper with each king, bit by bit with each compromise, until brazen idol worship engulfed the entire nation, starting with the leader of God's people. But an ember of hope remained.

God was not finished with Israel. His promise to Abraham remained because God is faithful even when His people are not. Elijah knew his place in God's kingdom. Elijah was God's prophet, and that flame would soon roar to life and grow into a mighty signal fire on Mount Carmel that would lead the way back to God and encourage those who remained faithful to God's Word to come out of the shadows.

The word "brave" in 1 Corinthians 16:13 comes from the Greek word *andrizomai* (Strong's G407). The word translates to "act like a man," and this is the only place in the Bible in which this word is used. Elijah was God's man. Elijah was a preacher, and I know firsthand that a preacher's gotta preach! Elijah knew his spiritual gift and did what God made him do. Elijah was not the one who rained fire from heaven and did not shut up the skies. He proclaimed God's message. He did not wait for a king's invitation because God gave him the mandate. Elijah did his part. He did what God called him to do, and the power of God met him in the middle of that mandate.

God made me a preacher. I did not know it until I had to preach a sermon for my homiletics class in Bible college. I never wanted to be a preacher. I am serious. People ask me, "Why would you go to Bible college if you didn't want to be a preacher?" I went because I wanted to study the Bible, and I was excited to learn that there were colleges dedicated to nothing but studying the Bible. However, when I finished that sermon in class, I knew that God made me do this. I seize every opportunity to use my gift. I do not wait for an invitation. God opens up countless opportunities, and not just on Sundays or Wednesdays. My wife hears more sermons from me than anyone else. My staff knows if they open the door and give me a chance, I will preach; at the grocery store, the restaurant, pumping gas...anywhere, because God expects me to use my gift.

We are all called to be people of prayer. We all have the right name, Jesus. We all have the same mission: to represent the Lord. And we are all given a Spiritual gift. We do not all have the same gift, but they are all imparted by the same Holy Spirit to accomplish the work of the ministry. "Having then gifts differing according to the grace that is given to us, let us use them." (Romans 12:6)

We do not always know our Spiritual gift when God first saves us. I advise this: First, ask a pastor where they need help. Next, jump in and serve with humility, excellence, and faithfulness. No matter what our gifts are, we are all servants first. None of this comes naturally, but that is good because we depend on the love of God through the power of God. Elijah's people use their spiritual gifts to serve others. Spiritual gifts always elevate the name of Jesus Christ because that is what the Holy Spirit does. He points to the Gospel of Jesus Christ because that is the power of God for salvation. God desires to save people.

We engage our gift through the power of the Holy Spirit. We are motivated by God's love for people. It is all about reaching people, and love must be at the center of everything we do in the name of the Lord. Love often requires confrontation, and Jesus did not hesitate to confront when the situation demanded it.

"When He had made a whip of cords, He drove them all out of the temple, with the sheep and the oxen, and poured out the changers' money and overturned the tables." (John 2:15) Before Jesus reacted, He stopped and caught His breath while making a whip. He was bold. He was angry, but He was in control.

Our society has a problem. We overreact to overreactions on television, on social media, in our churches, and on our streets. Instead of taking time to catch our breath, we match their level of fury until the conflict goes nuclear, destroying families, churches, and even entire neighborhoods. I oftentimes want to overreact. I want to burn them up, but that is not what Jesus did, and He rebuked the disciples anytime they suggested it.

Hear me. I know we must confront the evil in our society. We use God's Word, but must pause, collect our thoughts, and ask God for His wisdom, discernment, and direction. We can heal destruction if we react with love, grace, and mercy in the face of hate, vengeance, and violence while still standing in God's Word's authority. Jesus knew how to lay aside His entitlement, wash feet, and serve from the day He stepped down from heaven to the day He laid down His own life.

ELIJAH FOLLOWED GOD

"Get away from here and turn eastward, and hide by the Brook Cherith, which flows into the Jordan." (1 Kings 17:3)

Elijah threw it down and was ready to finish what he started, but God pulled him back and sat him down. Elijah was a man of action, but God's will for him was to wait. God's decision to pull him away for a season did not make him any less called or chosen. In fact, it was because God chose him for such a mighty work that God knew it was essential to prepare him. If we attempt to do work for God before He has completed His work IN us, the work of God may destroy us. Rather than argue with God or provide a list of reasons why God should do it now and do it His way, Elijah yielded his will to the will of God. Elijah listened to God and followed His instructions. He had faith-faith in God's plan, in God's timing, and in God Himself.

Elijah, meń and women, understand that God's timing is always best, but it is often difficult, especially when he plans to *wait*. Especially when He says, "You're not yet ready." Trusting God when He says, "Wait" takes just as much faith as it does when He says, "Go." When Jesus saves us, He simply calls us. *Follow Me.* We start our new lives full of hope and expectation, eager to step into what God has for us. We do not know that as we follow the Lord, He works in us, transforming us until we look more and more like His Son. The world does not need to see and hear Bill Gehm. The world needs to see and hear the Holy Spirit, and the more I reflect on the Lord Jesus, the brighter my light becomes, and this world needs the Light of my Savior.

The scope of my work reaches far beyond what I even knew to ask for in 1972, when God saved me, but my call is unchanging. It is a simple calling; to shine the Light of Jesus wherever God sends me. He leads, and I follow, so whether it is "Go," "Wait," or "Stay," Elijah's people always follow God and trust His timing, His plan, and His will because we trust in God Himself.

Chapter Two

DEVELOPMENT - SANCTIFICATION

PULLED AWAY

My mom took me to church all the time when I was growing up, but as soon as I left the building, I never gave God a second thought. I had my life all mapped out, but I was headed in the wrong direction. When I was sixteen, what had been one of the worst weeks of my life, culminated in a motorcycle wreck as I flipped my motorcycle end over end down the side of a hill.

It certainly was not how I had planned to go down that hill, but it ended up being the best unplanned detour because God opened my eyes to the truth. Had I died that day, I would have gone to hell. I should have died, but God met me at the bottom of that wreckage so that He could save my soul. I knew then that my only hope was Jesus Christ, and I did not wait for the next church service. The dirt became my altar, and my knees hit the ground. I was done fighting with the Lord. I surrendered everything then and there.

I did not have much to offer the Lord, but I said, "Here I am, Lord."

God said, "I'll take it!"

The kid who hated reading could not read the Bible enough. I could not wait to go to church. A flame was lit that day, and the fire of God still burns in my soul even today. I could not wait to set the world on fire for Jesus. Salvation is freely given purely from God's love, grace, and mercy. The only part we play is to receive the gift through faith. We believe in our hearts and confess with our mouths that Jesus is Lord. At that moment, we receive eternal life. However, as if that were not enough, God graciously offers abundant life with our remaining time here on earth.

We are already set apart from the destruction, but being saved is about more than just being spared from eternal hell. God wants to set us apart for good works. Sanctification is a big word that simply means "set apart" for something special. God saved me when I was sixteen, but I did not look, walk, talk, or act like Jesus. The Lord did not expect me to, because I did not yet know His ways. All I knew was that I was a sinner headed for hell, and now I was headed for heaven. I was a saint but did not know what a saint was. Suddenly, my life counted for something more than me, myself, and I.

God does not demand perfection. He desires cooperation. Sanctification is a partnership. It is where the Holy Spirit and our cooperation meet. The Good News is that God is patient and persistent. He completes what He starts and takes His time to make it right.

"For we are His workmanship, created in Christ Jesus for good works, which God prepared beforehand that we should walk in them." (Ephesians 2:10)

The Lord prepared some beautiful works for my future—my wife, my children and grandchildren, my church, and the radio station—but I was not yet prepared for them. God first had to work in me. God's ways will never make sense because they are much higher than ours. He told us that. God always tells the truth, so the process must start with His Word.

"Then the word of the LORD came to him, saying, 'Get away from here and turn eastward, and hide by the Brook Cherith which flows into the Jordan.'" (1 Kings 17:2-3)

God's word is a mirror. It shows us the truth about who God is and reflects our nature back to us. We see the part that looks like Him and the parts that need some work. The Word of God came to Elijah. It instructed him. It guided him. He knew he was God's man, and Elijah was ready to go now. As ready and determined as Elijah was, Baal had a stronghold on Israel. God's man needed to know just how mighty, faithful, and unfailing his God was, especially before he took on a showdown with the enemy of God's people. God has no obligation to prove Himself to anyone, but He does so willingly, not for His benefit but ours.

As we follow God, we learn He is exactly who He says He is, and we can trust Him. We let go of our own wisdom and understanding and absorb His ways as our ways. As we adopt His ways, we start to look like Him. We reflect Him and bring light into the darkest corners of the world, exposing the enemy and the works of darkness. The enemy is strong, smart, and well-connected, but not stronger or smarter than the Lord. Our God has infinite resources, and He has already defeated the enemy. When we let go of our own wisdom and understanding, our sin, and our doubts, we make room for the supernatural power of the Holy Spirit to work in us and flow through us. Elijah had amazing supernatural works of God in his future.

God could see the big picture, and Elijah may not have known that as God pulled him away to prepare him for what was coming, He was also preparing the hearts of Israel. The heavens dried up. There was no rain. There was only famine, drought, and death. God was using this time to make Israel hungry and thirsty literally. He was making them desperate. Their problem went much deeper than a lack of rain. Hunger and thirst were just symptoms of their lack, not just food and water, but of the Word and the Spirit of God. It was so much greater than just preparing Elijah. God was showing Israel that their lack was due to their rejection of Israel's one and only God, who had protected and provided for them for so long. God used these three years to make Israel desperate. He used these three years to make Elijah ready. God would meet Israel in that desperation through this prophet to bring Israel back to Himself.

Before He could do all of those works through me, the Lord had to do a work in me. I had to be removed from my desires, agenda, and plans so that He could set me apart for His design. I had to be emptied so that I could be filled with His desires, the Holy Spirit, faith, hope, and love. The Lord had to develop my character so that I could represent Him well as a husband, a father, a grandfather, a pastor, and a man of God. It is not just a one-time deal. The Lord spends our entire lives refining and developing us so that we may look more and more like Him.

Too many voices clamor for our attention, and it is easy to drown out God's voice. We must learn to prioritize God's voice above all others. The Word says faith comes by hearing, and hearing by the Word of God. (Romans 10:17)

One of the most important steps we take in our development is to learn to get away with God and His Word. Our relationship with God is our most important ministry. We give Him our time, hearts, minds, and attention, and He gives us His Word, Spirit, and presence. Everything we do flows from that source.

So often, we put everything else ahead of God until God becomes our last resort.

God pulled Elijah away so that He could train him to trust in Him first—for his provision, his fellowship, and his strength. People are fickle. The earth will pass away. God alone is unfailing and faithful. His well will never run dry. God brought many people into Elijah's life to minister to and help him, but the most important truth Elijah had to learn—the most important thing any of us can learn- is that God is all we need. He is all sufficient.

THE BROOK CHERITH-THE PLACE OF CUTTING

For some people, myself included, isolation with God near a brook does not sound so bad. I could easily see myself holed up in a cabin in the Rocky Mountains with my wife, Bible, and God. A quiet place near a brook sounds perfect until we realize what God really wants to do.

Cherith is a word that means to cut or separate. Remember our word at the beginning, sanctification? God set Elijah apart because he wanted to prepare him for a special purpose. God would reveal Himself to Israel in a mighty way through Elijah. God had to prepare Elijah, which meant some things had to be removed, even some things he held dear.

We come into this deal with a list of prejudices, wounds, and addictions. We are connected to the vine that is Jesus Christ, but the dead branches must be cut away, or they will choke the life out of any fruit that tries to grow there. They are dead weight, and they need to be pruned.

A BIRD-BRAINED IDEA

"And it will be that you shall drink from the brook, and I have commanded the ravens to feed you there." (1 Kings 17:4)

"The ravens brought him bread and meat in the morning, and bread and meat in the evening; and he drank from the brook." (1 Kings 17:6)

Elijah could not accept food from ravens, could he? Elijah was a Jewish man, and Jewish people could not have anything to do with unclean birds, right? Elijah had a choice to make. He could refuse the bread and meat because the Law told him to abstain. If Elijah refused the food, he would die of starvation, for there were no other resources.

His other choice was to accept what God was offering, whether or not it made sense to him. Hear me when I say I am not talking about violating God's Word. On the contrary, the Lord decided that He would use ravens to provide for Elijah.

Elijah chose to trust God. He did not have to understand how or why God chose to use the ravens. He simply had to trust the Lord. The ravens came at just the right time, in just the right place, and in just the right amount because even these unclean birds were under the authority and Lordship of God Almighty. Reasoning and understanding did not bring the ravens every day. Trust and obedience did.

I followed God to Amarillo, Texas in 1980, when a church hired me to be their youth pastor. That church had serious problems, and I questioned the Lord many times. *How could you have brought me here? How can I possibly learn anything from this place? Maybe I heard your voice all wrong!* I prayed so many times for God to let me leave, but He insisted that I stay, and God used that church to prune the dead branches in me. God provided for me every week as that crazy church paid my salary. I was thankful for the provision from those "unclean birds." I depended on them to provide for me and my family, and God kept His promises. He never left me.

He took some things away, but He also provided. He gave me more children and new friends. I rely on Him to sustain me. God uses "unclean birds" in our lives all the time. They are called people, and God provided seventeen people to help start what would become Grace Church.

How were we going to start a church? None of us knew how. None of us were official "church planters." We did not know how, when, or even where, but we knew we had God. We had His Word. We had seventeen people who were willing to follow God. It worked, and God provided for us, step by step, exactly when, where, and who we would need at any given time. He never let us down, and His presence is still with Grace Church as it grows greater than any of us could have imagined.

People are messy, and getting involved with them will make our lives messy. God employs those people to prune and provide for us. Be thankful for your boss, no matter what kind of boss he or she is. Be patient and faithful because God is always working in every season. Do not give up before God is finished.

Elijah did not leave the brook until God told him it was time to go. Our nature is to pull back from anything painful, but if God had given me what I wanted, if he had released me from Amarillo, Grace Church would have never happened in my life. He would have given it to someone else.

Our religious understanding and reasoning can sometimes get in the way of what God wants. God simply does not do things as we think He should. And even if we are so schooled in the letter of God's Word, His ways still, and will always, mystify us, and we have to be okay with that. We must be okay with knowing and trusting that the Lord's way is always the best. As the Holy Spirit prunes away our need to understand and control every situation, we come under His authority and Lordship. We trust Him with all of our hearts, and not our understanding. (Proverbs 3:5) Our religious practices will not sustain us in a barren land. It is our relationship with the Lord.

Just because God moves in ways that do not align with our reasoning does not mean he has not orchestrated them. The Pharisees clung to a specific image of how they thought the Messiah should look, and when Jesus came, He looked nothing like that. They missed who was standing right in front of them. Jesus told them repeatedly, "I am the Bread of Life," but they still refused what He offered. They starved to death spiritually when they did not have to. They just had to trust Him.

Lord, prune us, cut away our need and desire to understand and control everything. Open our eyes to see and our ears to hear. Open our hearts to recognize when You move. Please help us to be like Elijah. Help us follow, trust, obey, and receive all You have for us.

WHEN THE BROOK DRIES UP

Sometimes we become so accustomed to God's miracles that we can take Him for granted. We figure out how to build a cabin by the brook. We may even start to think we can do God's work in our own strength with our own hands. So, what if the ravens stop coming? We can learn to fish. Life has become a pleasant routine, so *why would we move now*?

God knows our nature. He knows that if we get too comfortable, we will never move, so sometimes, He has to remove our blanket of complacency to make us get up and start moving. Elijah learned to live by the brook. He was even thriving. It was not a bad place at all. The ravens kept coming. The Lord kept teaching. Why would he ever want to leave? God did not want Elijah to settle down at the brook. He tried to take Elijah to the top of a mountain.

"And it happened after a while that the brook dried up, because there had been no rain in the land." (1 Kings 17:7)

The brook dried up because it stopped raining. God was doing exactly what Elijah prayed for. He closed the heavens. It was not a punishment. It was confirmation that Elijah was exactly where he was supposed to be.

Seasons change. Right now, I am a pastor. Someday, I might not be. Choose something; our wealth, youth, popularity, health, and so on. It is all going to eventually dry up. But as long as we are following the Lord, we will be exactly where God wants us to be, and He is the one thing that will never dry up. No matter what season we are in, we are still His people, and He is still our God. Our titles will change, but our identity never does. We are His children, and He is our Father. He is a good Father who always knows how to care for His children.

What do we do when the brook dries up? We praise God. We remember that the Lord gives and takes away. We always say, "Blessed be the name of the Lord" because our God never changes, even when seasons do.

ZAREPHATH-THE PLACE OF REFINING

We are just passing through, and at no point are we supposed to become so attached to anything in this world that it would cause us to stop moving forward to our destination in heaven. The Lord leads, and we follow. How closely we follow is up to us. If we follow closely, we will discover that God's Word and His blessings are not just about us.

"Then the word of the LORD came to him, saying, 'Arise, go to Zarephath, which belongs to Sidon, and dwell there. See, I have commanded a widow there to provide for you.'" (1 Kings 17:8-9)

Elijah's journey began in a secret place. It was just Him and Elijah. He took Elijah to school and to a holy training ground. Elijah learned to hear God's voice. He learned to depend on Him. He learned that God was the provider and sustainer of life, but Elijah's call was about more than just himself. It always is. God's goal is to redeem people, and a desperate widow in Zarephath needed the saving hand of God. Elijah did not mourn the good old days when God sent the ravens. God sent a new word for a new season.

BEHIND ENEMY LINES

Baal worship originated in Sidon. What business could a prophet of God possibly have in the heart of Baal territory? It was God's business because God told Elijah, "I have chosen a widow." God frequently chooses people whom the world discards. Their need for Him attracts him because He can reveal His glory through them. The Lord proved to Elijah that all creation, even the birds named unclean, are subject to God's will and authority. It is interesting to see how God built upon that lesson. God sent Elijah to the center of Baal worship. God would show that He is sovereign, even on the enemy's own turf. Nowhere was off limits for God's hand to move, and God would provide for His prophet and rescue a widow and her son.

God sent me, a mountain-loving man, from the heart of the Rocky Mountains to Amarillo, Texas. Amarillo is hot, dry, and windy. Sometimes it looks like a wilderness. It is full of rednecks, but guess what? God loves those rednecks, and they need someone to share the hope of the Gospel. Over and over, I watch the Word of God and the Spirit of God meet in people's hearts, and I watch God flip the switch as they make the connection between their head and their heart. I get to see them grow into Godly men and women. I live for those moments and am so glad I did not say *no* when God told me to go.

Clean versus unclean does not seem like such a big deal when we are talking about birds, but how often do we mark certain groups of people as lost causes or avoid certain places because we are convinced that they are so far gone or so deep in the enemy's grasp that God's hand cannot reach out and deliver? The Holy Spirit clearly warned the Apostle Peter in Acts 10 not to call anyone or anything unclean that God had set aside for Himself. We do not get to decide. God does not wish for anyone to perish.

Jesus asked a Samaritan woman for a drink. He asked a tax collector to have lunch with Him. Jesus reached out to those whom the spiritual elite wrote off as unfit or unworthy. Jesus used them to meet His physical needs and shared the bread of life with them until He met their greatest need as a Savior.

That is what Jesus does. We were all sinners, lost, and unclean until Jesus reached down and sent someone our way with the hope of salvation. We are washed clean by the blood of the Lamb. The power of the Gospel transforms us.

GOD CHOSE A WIDOW

The Widow replied, "As the LORD your God lives, I do not have bread, only a handful of flour in a bin, and a little oil in a jar; and see, I am gathering a couple of sticks that I may go in and prepare it for myself and my son, that we may eat it, and die." (1 Kings 17:12)

Right away, we learn that the widow from Zarephath had only enough provisions for one more meal for herself and her son. After that, she was preparing to die. To the world's eyes, she was helpless and useless. She had nothing to offer anyone, much less the prophet of God. However, God saw this widow, and He chose her. He knew exactly where she was, exactly what she had, and precisely what she needed. God does not lose track of anyone. He sees the widow, the orphan, the single parent, the young, the old, the weak, the strong, and everyone in between. He sees them all. He leaves the 99 to find the one lost soul in need of Him, and He has plans for them.

I am pretty sure God's strategy looked nothing like what Elijah had envisioned for himself the day he dropped his challenge in Ahab's courts, but God had a proven track record. It is unlikely that a Gentile widow from Baal country could have anything to offer. However, it was unlikely that ravens could know where, when, and how much food to bring to Elijah, but they did, every single day, just like God had said. And, when Elijah arrived in Zarephath, there was the widow, just as God said. God always does what He says, and this was no chance encounter. The Lord ordained this meeting.

"So he arose and went to Zarephath. And when he came to the gate of the city, a widow was there gathering sticks. And he called to her and said, 'Please bring me a little water in a cup, that I may drink." (1 Kings 17:10)

Elijah talked to the widow. He did not just live a good life and hoped his example would be enough to win her over. Hear me when I say that being a Godly example is good, but at some point, we must engage the people God has placed in our lives. The Holy Spirit already marked this widow. God created a hunger in her life before the prophet ever arrived. She was in a desperate, hopeless place.

The Holy Spirit always goes before us, drawing people to Himself and preparing their hearts to receive His message. Sometimes, fear of rejection will discourage us from engaging the people around us. Still, honestly, in light of the eternal stakes, their rejection, even their mocking, is worth the risk because their soul literally hangs in the balance. Who cares if they reject or mock us because the men and women who listen to our message, even if only one, are worth it.

"And as she was going to get it, he called to her and said, 'Please bring me a morsel of bread in your hand." (1 Kings 17:11)

Elijah connected with this widow. She was open to his request because God had put His mark on her, and because the widow gave him an opening, Elijah decided to go all in with what he knew about her, himself, and the Lord.

"And as she was going to get it, he called her and said, 'Please bring me a morsel of bread in your hand. So, she said, 'As the Lord your God lives, I do not have bread, only a handful of flour in a bin, and a little oil in a jar; and see, I am gathering a couple of sticks that I may go in and prepare it for myself and my son, that we may eat it, and die." (1 Kings 17:11-12)

We never know the burdens people carry unless we take the time to talk to them. The widow planned to go into her house, eat, then prepare to die, just her and her son. She'd reached the end of herself. She did everything she knew to do, hoping it would be enough, but her best efforts came up short. It did not matter how much she rationed, what she had, or how hard she worked day after day. Once the supply ran out, it was gone, and all that was left was death. Elijah picked a bad day to show up, or maybe, by God's grace, this was the perfect day to show up.

"And Elijah said to her, 'Do not fear, go and do as you have said, but make me a small cake from it first, and bring it to me, and afterward make some for yourself and your son.

For thus says the LORD God of Israel: "The bin of flour shall not be used up, nor shall the jar of oil run dry, until the day the LORD sends the rain on the earth." (1 Kings 17:13-14)

Elijah already knew God could provide something from nothing because He had already done so with the ravens. Elijah knew God would provide for the widow because He revealed to Elijah that He was going to use the widow to take care of him. Three days after I moved to Amarillo to be the youth pastor, my senior pastor, an "old" man in his 40s, assigned me a task.

"Bill, I'm entrusting you with a group of widows." He then took me to a retirement community where five to fifteen widows gathered. I thought to myself, "Wait a minute! I'm the youth pastor. Let me take care of the young people and maybe those up to their thirties, but you're the senior pastor. You take care of the widows."

I did not say any of that, but I thought it. Soon, I would realize that widows were part of God's plan for me, and to this day, He has yet to release me from preaching to widows.

The widow at Zarephath had a choice to make. She had everything to lose by saying yes, and she had everything to gain by saying yes. Here was a man she had never met pleading with her to believe in a God she had never heard of. If she did what Elijah asked of her, she risked wasting the last of her resources, and death would come even sooner than she had planned. If she moved ahead with her own plan, death was still certain.

She knew that day after day she did the same thing, but in the end, it came up short. The prophet's words offered hope for the first time in a long time, and it may have seemed foolish, but she stepped out in faith and released what she had into the hands of the Lord.

"So, she went away and did according to the word of Elijah; and she and he and her household ate for many days. The flour bin was not used up, nor did the jar of oil run dry, according to the word of the Lord, which He spoke by Elijah." (1 Kings 17:15-16)

God used Elijah to speak life into death and bring hope into desperation. Make no mistake. God's Word had power, but He moved through the man Elijah. God was the source, and Elijah was a vessel.

The widow started her fire that day with the sticks she gathered, and everything moved from the Word of God spoken to the Word of God in action. It was not enough for the widow to believe; she had to put action behind her faith. God met her in her need when she offered everything, she had to Him. He became her all-sufficient Provider. Neither the flour nor the oil ran out, and not just enough for her and her son, but also for the man of God. Abundant life. God brought life and restored hope during a drought, and God's Word saved them both. God's Word sustained them both.

The Holy Spirit marks people all the time. Every week, the widows met with me for Bible study. Five years into my ministry with them, I told them, "We're starting a new church."

God used them to pray for me and encourage me. One widow, Noma, had three sons. Noma passed away about a year after I started Grace Church. As her sons were making funeral arrangements, they remembered their mother talking about the "crazy" preacher who ministered to her each week. They called and asked me if I would officiate at her funeral. When I arrived to meet with them, they thought I was the flower delivery guy!

I met Noma's youngest son, Dennis. Dennis had been hurt in church, discouraged by a brook that dried up. Over time, he allowed God's Word to revive him and bring back to life what was once dead. God marked him. I just showed up with His Word. Dennis was fundamental in launching our radio station, Radio by Grace, which now reaches nationwide. He poured into my life. Together, we poured into others-people we may never know or meet this side of heaven. It was a blessed partnership, much like Elijah and the widow. We watched the Gospel go "Boom!" in so many lives.

Jesus carried a cross made from two wooden beams, representing death. Jesus obeyed God's Word. Genesis 3:15 promised a Savior would come, and hope became realized when that first nail hit those sticks. Death made way to eternal life, and the promise of hope came true.

WHEN THE UNTHINKABLE HAPPENS

"Now it happened after these things that the son of the woman who owned the house became sick. And his sickness was so serious that there was no breath left in him." (1 Kings 17:17)

Sometimes, life does not add up. The unthinkable happens. We follow the Lord, trust Him, obey His Word, and live a life of faith, but the truth is that we will not be spared from trials. God did not spare His own Son, and Jesus warned us that we would have many trials in this world. It is going to be tough. But, in that same verse, He gives us hope: "I have overcome the world."

Sanctification is never about becoming so proficient in our faith that we become independent from God. On the contrary, the more we grow in Him, the more we realize that we cannot even breathe without Him. He sustains us, and we learn to depend on Him for everything. Jesus Christ is our only hope because everything else comes and goes, even the loved ones we hold dear in our hearts.

What hope is there apart from Jesus? The answer is that there is none, but I can absolutely say without hesitation that after following Jesus in both good and bad times, I cling to Him more than I ever have. He is an everlasting and enduring hope that will carry us to the end because He has overcome the world.

That does not mean that trials will not hurt. Some trials will knock the breath right out of us and make us question everything we know. The widow was new in her faith. She did everything right. She obeyed the Lord. She surrendered her life and her son's life to the Lord because she emptied everything she had at His request.

She lived a life of faith, but the unthinkable happened in the middle of everything. Her only son died. What good was it to trust God if He was going to let her son die anyway? Those of us who are parents know that it would be easier if the trials happened to us rather than our children, but here she was. It seemed all hope had been lost. Now what was she to do?

“So she asked Elijah, "What have I to do with you, O man of God? Have you come to me to bring my sin to remembrance, and to kill my son?" (1 Kings 17:18)

When people get mad at God, they call the preacher. I have sat in hospital rooms, funeral homes, and beside gravesides with people who are trying to make sense of what does not add up. Sometimes, they lash out. They come at me with their questions, and I could lecture them about the sovereignty of God, but theology does not ease the suffering of a grieving mother. The truth is, I do not have an answer, and most of the time, even if I did have the perfect answer to their questions, they would not want to hear it anyway.

I know the Lord cares about our grief and is close to the brokenhearted. I know that the Holy Spirit is our comfort, and the best thing we can do is carry them before the Lord in prayer.

"And he said to her, ‘Give me your son.’ So he took him out of her arms and carried him to the upper room where he was staying, and laid him on his own bed." (1 Kings 17:19)

Elijah did not try to explain the Lord or defend His actions or lack thereof. He did ask to share in her grief and to help carry this burden. He carried the burden with him until he could release it into the hands of the Lord. Elijah cared about the widow and wanted to help, but he could do nothing.

I have been there with members of my congregation as they look to me for help amid their worst nightmares. To be invited into someone's grief is to be invited onto holy ground. We do not preach the theology of suffering. We do not quote Romans 8:28, "All things work together for good", to someone who just buried their loved one. We simply sit with them, love them, and trust that the Lord will keep His promise to be near them. The only thing I know to do is to bring them before my Father in prayer. It really is the most powerful and spiritual thing we can do. Elijah struggled with questions but saved them for his prayer closet, alone with his God.

"O LORD my God, have You also brought tragedy on the widow with whom I lodge, by killing her son?" (1 Kings 17:20)

The Good News is that Jesus knows exactly how to minister to those in their darkest places because He is well acquainted with grief. Isaiah 53:3 tags Him as the Man of Sorrows. Jesus knew the cross was coming for Him, and He invited His closest disciples into the Garden of Gethsemane, where He agonized before the Father in prayer, and the depth of His despair grieved them. They tried to hang with Him, but the weight of eternity bore down on His shoulders, and it was too much for them to carry. There was nothing they could do for Him.

The weight of trying to carry, in my own strength, the burdens of my family, my staff, my congregation, and my own personal burdens will crush me, so I bring them to the One who has already borne all of my burdens. I don't have the answers, but I do have THE answer. I have prayers and know my heavenly Father hears me when I call out to Him. He always answers my prayers-sometimes with yes, sometimes with no, and sometimes with not now, but always according to His will. No matter what His answer may be, I know that He is always with me. I know

He is always with the people I love; that is my answer to life when the unimaginable happens.

"And he stretched himself out on the child three times, and cried out to the LORD and said, O LORD my God, I pray, let this child's soul come back to him." (1 Kings 17:21)

Elijah knew his request sounded impossible, but why not ask for the impossible? He had already asked God to shut up the heavens and hold back the rains. He watched God send the ravens. He tasted the bread made with flour and oil, which never ran out. There was nothing too hard for God, and Elijah did not just pray once and move on.

He reached out and connected with the boy. He kept asking, he kept praying, and the Lord gave him exactly what he asked for.

"Then the LORD heard the voice of Elijah; and the soul of the child came back to him, and he revived." (1 Kings 17:22)

Do not stop praying for people. Keep asking. Keep seeking. Keep knocking on God's door. Keep reaching out and connecting until something happens. I have one request before the Lord that I have prayed about every single day for the past several years. When will I stop? Not until God answers or until I am in heaven. I know that God can bring resurrection power into any situation that we thought was dead, hopeless, and ready to be buried.

"And Elijah said, 'See, your son lives' "Then the woman said to Elijah, 'Now by this I know that you are a man of God, and that the word of the LORD in your mouth is the truth.'" (1 Kings 17:23-24)

God brought salvation to the widow and her son. They were destined to starve to death, but God sent Elijah with the Bread of Life. Resurrection power revived what was dead and removed all doubt from the widow's heart. She had hope and a future because she knew that Elijah's God was real and that His Word could be trusted. The Lord chose to reveal Himself to this widow through the Prophet of God.

We were all like this widow woman, dead in our trespasses, doing the same thing day after day in our own power and strength, knowing full well that someday it would no longer be enough. But God sent the message of hope into our lives, and He took us from death to life. Now, we carry this message with us everywhere we go.

The Prophet of God was a man with a nature just like ours, but he carried with him the message of power and hope. The Lord God of Israel lived. We carry the message of hope with us too. According to Romans, the Gospel is God's power for salvation, Hebrews says Jesus is our living hope.

IT'S GO TIME

God had spent the last three years preparing Elijah for his message on Mount Carmel. Elijah became rooted in his faith. He knew God heard and answered his prayers. He knew he would not face Carmel alone because God was with him everywhere he went.

What if Elijah did not have enough? Enough strength, enough courage, enough faith?

That was okay because God was the source. He watched God take a single supply of oil and flour and turn it into abundance.

What if Elijah died on top of the mountain? Elijah did not fear death because he had experienced resurrection power with the widow's son. God's Word had the final say, not death.

We know Jesus promised He would never leave or forsake us, and Jesus always keeps His promises. We know that when we place our trust in Jesus, a little becomes a lot. We know that Jesus overcame death, and death does not have the final word. Jesus already had the last word.

Elijah was ready to declare to the entire nation of Israel that their God was still alive and well. Their God was the only God.

We live to declare that Jesus Christ is alive and well, and He will save all who call upon the name of the Lord. We know it is go time, and we pray, "Lord, here I am! Send me!"

Chapter Three

DESTINY

THE MOUNTAIN

IT CAME TO PASS

"And it came to pass after many days that the Word of the LORD came to Elijah, in the third year saying, 'Go, present yourself to Ahab, and I will send rain on the earth.'" (1 Kings 18:1)

Every word recorded in the Bible has either already come true, is coming true, or will come true in the future. Where? When? How? That is all up to the Lord. Heaven and earth will come to pass, but God's Word will endure forever. That is why we do not anchor ourselves to anything else but the Lord and His Word. Everything is as shifting as the sand, but the Word of God is an everlasting foundation because it is built on Jesus Christ. Israel exists because God chose them to be His people. Israel endures because God's promises endure. "For I am the LORD, I do not change; Therefore you are not consumed, O sons of Jacob." (Malachi 3:6) God finishes what He starts, and He does not give up on His people. He is always faithful, even when we are disloyal to Him.

When I preach, I always pray that the Lord will communicate His Word to the hearts of those who listen, whether it is the man or woman sitting in our sanctuary or the truck driver who is driving across I-40 listening to Radio By Grace. For some people, their hearts open right away, and they respond immediately. For others, it takes a bit more time. I keep preaching as faithfully and accurately as I know how, and I watch hearts soften week after week until suddenly it comes to pass and their day of salvation arrives. The power is in God's Word. The timing is in God's hands.

It was finally "go" time for Elijah. He spent the past three years following the Lord, consistently growing and faithfully serving where he was. It came to pass that Elijah would have his showdown on Mount Carmel.

God said it was "go" time when I went to Bible College. I met my wife there. We moved from Michigan to Colorado and then to Amarillo, Texas. I am still the pastor at Grace Church, and I am still on the go. So is our church. We moved from a lock shop to our own building. We moved from that building to the old grocery store on Western and Plains. We launched Radio By Grace. We helped build an orphanage in Africa.

It sounds exhausting because it was. It sounds exciting because it is! I would do it all again because following God is the most thrilling ride we can take. We can stop and admire the shiny sports car, but that is not the same thing as getting in, buckling up, and going for a ride.

It is the most fulfilling way we can spend our time on earth. What else is there to live for? Me? Myself and I? Everything fades away. It will come to pass. Only the Kingdom of God lasts forever, so we spend our days building His Kingdom, and His Kingdom is all about people.

We cannot allow the church to become a museum where we stop and marvel at past historical works. Yes, they happened, and we are grateful for every great move of God, but we are expected to move forward and build on those works. We are still a living and moving force because we are the church of the Living God. There are still people who need to be saved, and God did not place us in the past. He placed us here and now, and we are still commanded to "Go therefore and make disciples of all the nations, baptizing them in the name of the Father and of the Son and of the Holy Spirit." (Matthew 28:19)

Someday, the work will cease. The time to rest and reflect will come when we can sit down with our Savior and the saints gathered around Him. Then we can tell of the wonderful things the Lord did in our lives. We will marvel at the face of Jesus. But, until then, we go!

SECRET AGENT MAN

"And Ahab had called Obadiah, who was in charge of his house. (Now Obadiah feared the LORD greatly. For it was while Jezebel massacred the prophets of the LORD, that Obadiah had taken one hundred prophets and hidden them, fifty to a cave, and had fed them with bread and water.)" (1 Kings 18:3–4)

What about me, Pastor Bill? I am not called to preach. I am never going to start a radio station. I am a secretary, or a farmer, or a doctor, or a parent. Where does a person with a regular job fit into this Kingdom?

The Good News is that if we want to be used by God, He will most assuredly use us, and the list of qualifications that He looks for in a man or woman of God is different for each of us.

Hidden within this huge story of the mighty prophet Elijah, the Bible introduces us to another man, whose name is Obadiah.

His name means "Servant of Jehovah". That is it. That is the only qualification God looks for in a man or woman of God. They simply have to be His servants. They say "Yes" to whatever the Master requests of them, and God called upon Obadiah for an important task in His Kingdom.

Just as God has plans, His enemy has plans too. They both use people who are willing to do their bidding. The enemy of God sought to remove the Name and the Word of God from Israel forever, not only destroying God's people but also trying to stop the plans for our future Redeemer. Satan remembered God's promise way back in the Garden of Eden to stomp on the head of the serpent. Sadly, the enemy found a more than willing vessel in Ahab's wife, Jezzy, and when Elijah confronted Ahab and his wife for the first time, they doubled their efforts to hunt down and destroy the prophets.

THE RIGHT MAN IN THE WRONG PLACE

God pulled Elijah away to hide him and protect him from the enemy's wrath, but He left behind a man hidden in plain sight. Obadiah took upon himself the burden of hiding one hundred prophets of Israel right under the king's nose. Obadiah was Ahab's house manager. He had a regular job, but God needed someone who could protect all of those prophets, and God chose Obadiah right where he was. Obadiah was just as called. He was anointed by the same Holy Spirit, and the Holy Spirit empowered Obadiah to carry out this work.

Obadiah did not try to imitate Elijah, nor did he envy Elijah's gift. He knew what God wanted him to do, and he surrendered his heart, his life, and his resources to the call of God to subvert the plans of the enemy. His story does not seem as big as Elijah's, but he was not unnoticed by God, and God placed him in the middle of Elijah's story for a reason.

The greatness of our works is not measured by the scale of their earthly impact. They are measured by the greatness of the God we serve and the everlasting impact they have on His Kingdom. God notices every single servant who obeys His Word and answers His call. Hebrews 11 is filled with a list of names, some famous and some less famous, but all giants of the faith because their faith is in our great God. Christmas day is coming for all of us, and we will receive our rewards. Our works may never be known on this side of heaven, but one day they will be revealed and commended by God in front of everyone.

Maybe we do have a wicked boss. Maybe we are the only believers at school. That is a hard place to be. Sometimes, it is a dangerous place to be, but it could be that God planted us there to accomplish His work and destroy the plans of the enemy.

How, when, and what that looks like are up to God. But know this: no matter how big or small, no matter if it goes viral or goes unnoticed by anyone around us, the same Holy Spirit empowers each of us. The scale of our works does not matter because when we give an account of the works we did do, they will have been done in the service of the Lord God Almighty. That is what we live for, or rather, that is Who we live for. Not that we do not all need a pat on the back from time to time, but hearing "Well done, good and faithful servant" from our Master will make everything worth it.

THE RIGHT MAN AT THE WRONG TIME

In the last part of Esther 4:14, Esther's uncle exhorts her to understand that she has "come to the kingdom for such a time as this." I would exhort us with the same reminder. God knew the political climate in which we would live. He knew the trials our world would face. He knew the various troubles that would plague the earth, and He decided when and where we would be born. We were designed and equipped for this time and this place, and we have the same weapons, strength, and power as all the saints we read about in scripture. We have the sword of the Spirit, which is God's Word. We have the strength of His name. We have the power of the Holy Spirit. God always has people to represent Him, and now is our time. It may seem like everything is stacked against us, and it is. The enemy has not changed, but neither has God, and God is for us.

Terror and suffering surrounded Obadiah. He witnessed the massacre of the prophets, but Obadiah "Feared the LORD" since his youth (1 Kings 18:12). Obadiah knew that, in spite of what he saw all around him, to choose the Lord's side was to choose the side of victory.

Obadiah started a cave ministry, hiding one hundred prophets inside two separate caves, fifty to a cave. He did not just hide them and leave them to fend for themselves. He cared for them, bringing food and water. God sent ravens to Elijah. He sent Obadiah to the other prophets, and both methods were part of God's plan.

Right after God saved me, an elderly woman named Corrie Ten Boom came to my church in Colorado and told her story. She and her family hid Jews during the Nazi invasion of Holland. God planted her family in the middle of darkness and suffering, and it cost them dearly. She wrote a book in 1971, The Hiding Place by Corrie Ten Boom with John and Elizabeth Sherrill detailing the events. She was sent to a concentration camp, but amid the horror, she was still "on the go" as she ministered to prisoners all around her. She survived, but most of her family died. The Jews she hid all survived. When she was released from the camp, she traveled the world to share the power of God's love. Her story began with her hiding eight to twelve people. It ended with her preaching to thousands, if not more, about the saving power of the Gospel of Jesus Christ.

WHAT IS YOUR STORY

Corrie, Elijah, and Obadiah—they all have amazing stories, but I want a story of my own. May we all desire our own stories with the Lord. How did we spend our time and resources? What did we risk? For whom did we care? Opportunities exist all around us—with our family, coworkers, classmates, and the people we encounter every day.

Lord, please open our eyes to see and our hearts to move.

Many men and women in my church have cave ministries. God called my wife to hold babies. She, along with other volunteers, care for and nurture babies in our nursery. They change dirty diapers and wipe snotty noses. Our children's church workers minister to children all the way from preschool to junior high. My youth pastor and numerous volunteers serve our junior high and high school students, and sometimes they act like cavemen.

Some go into prisons and hospitals. Some are prayer warriors who carry the burdens of the church in their hearts. My church could not survive without them, and I am thankful. They are neither forgotten nor unseen. God sees them. The Holy Spirit encourages them. No one stays in any ministry for long unless the Spirit meets them there. They all serve faithfully because they love and fear the Lord.

My executive pastor and his wife have fostered and adopted several children. The process has been overwhelming, hard, and inconvenient. It is costly. I have seen their hearts break, and I know it is painful. They surrender their sleep, their comfort, their resources, and their hearts. They love those children and do it because they submitted to God's call to go where no one else would go. God made them for this, and they have an amazing story. Their children are part of my family and part of the Gehm story.

SUBMISSION: THE OTHER "S" WORD

"And Ahab said to Obadiah, 'Go into the land to all the springs of water and to all the brooks; perhaps we may find grass to keep the horses and mules alive, so that we will not have to kill any livestock.' So they divided the land between them to explore it; Ahab went one way by himself, and Obadiah went the other way by himself." (1 Kings 18:5-6)

It seems contradictory that we would talk about Obadiah's submission when we already established that Ahab was firmly entrenched in the enemy's plan. However, we previously saw that Ahab was not the enemy. He was a puppet in the hands of the enemy. However, he was still king of Israel and Obadiah's employer. This was a prime example of someone living in the world but not being of this world.

Everyone hates the word "submission" because it goes against our nature. However, when we come under the Lordship of Jesus Christ, our lives become all about submission. The Lord Himself submitted: to His Father, to the Word, and even to other people when the Holy Spirit led Him to do so. He allowed John the Baptist to baptize Him. He washed the disciples' feet. He submitted Himself to the arresting soldiers when they came to take Him away. He even submitted Himself to death on a cross.

When we submit to those in authority, whether it be our bosses, our teachers, our spouses, or even our politicians, we are not submitting to "the man". We are submitting to the Lord. We work for the Lord.

"Whatever you do, do it heartily, as unto the Lord and not to men." (Colossians 3:23)

I am not talking about violating the Word of God. That is a different sermon for a different day. When Obadiah submitted to his boss, Ahab, he was not violating God's Word. He was still hiding the prophets. He was still preserving and protecting God's Word, but Obadiah did what his boss asked of him.

Ahab's people starved, but his priority was making sure the animals were cared for. Are not people worth more than animals? We are not the first generation on earth to deal with corrupt politicians and greedy bosses. Is it not important to govern with integrity? Do people not matter more than the bottom line? Are we not supposed to protect the innocent?

I know we are all frustrated because our leaders' priorities are all messed up. They have crazy ideas.

"What should we do, Pastor Bill?"

We submit.

We listen to the words of Peter in his first letter to the church, and we submit to our masters. I am not talking about when we are asked to violate God's Word. I am talking about submitting to those who are over us and doing the best job we can for them—not for their sake but for the sake of the Gospel. We work as if we are working for the Lord because the truth is, from the moment we clocked in as followers of Christ, we chose to represent the Lord in everything we do.

Obadiah may have hated his job, but it provided him with the means to care for the prophets. He may have had the worst boss, but he did a good job anyway. Ahab trusted Obadiah, and it was Ahab's trust in him that enabled Obadiah to hide the prophets right under his nose. Obadiah served God by submitting to Ahab, and it was on his road to submission that Obadiah and Elijah's paths intersected.

"Now as Obadiah was on his way, suddenly Elijah met him; and he recognized him, and fell on his face, and said, 'Is that you, my lord Elijah?'" (1 Kings 18:7)

DIFFERENT ROLES IN THE SAME STORY

Obadiah and Elijah walked on different roads for the past three years, but they were both serving the same God faithfully. It came to pass for Elijah, but it also came to pass for Obadiah. God had been preparing everyone for what was about to happen, not just Elijah.

"It is I. Go, tell your master, 'Elijah is here.'" (1 Kings 18:8)

By now, Obadiah's cave ministry ran like a machine. It was difficult and challenging, but it was familiar and comfortable because he did it all in secret. God hid Elijah. It did not turn out so well for Israel the first time Elijah went before Ahab, and Obadiah watched things go from bad to worse when Elijah disappeared. Obadiah was afraid.

"And it shall come to pass, as soon as I am gone from you, that the Spirit of the LORD will carry you to a place I do not know;" (1 Kings 18:12a)

Being associated with Elijah was a calculated risk that could cost Obadiah not only his life, but also the lives of the prophets that he had hidden away from Ahab and Jezzy. Everything he worked for could be lost.

Even if we lose it all, the Lord Jesus is worth the risk. He has already sacrificed everything for us. However, Jesus promised in Matthew 16:25 that even if we lose our lives for His sake, we would find them.

God wanted to reveal Himself to Israel, and Elijah encouraged Obadiah with the promise that he would be there, just like he said he would.

"Then Elijah said, 'As the LORD of hosts lives, before whom I stand, I will surely present myself to him today.'" (1 Kings 18:15)

Obadiah would not be left hanging. His brother in the faith would be there with him, and more importantly, the Lord would be there with them both.

Jesus encourages us with the same kind of promise. Take a chance on Him. Give everything to Him because it profits us nothing if we hang onto everything and lose our own soul. Jesus promised, that "the Son of Man will come in the glory of His Father with His angels, and then He will reward each according to His works". (Matthew 16:27)

Take the risk. Stand and be counted among the people of God. Stand for the Word of God. Jesus will not abandon us or leave us hanging. He will walk with us each step of the way while we wait for His return. And He is coming back with everything He promised.

WE NEED EACH OTHER

We need each other. We need people in the caves who faithfully care for God's Work day after day.

To those who labor each day in prayer behind closed doors, to the fathers and mothers who are raising their children in the ways of the Lord, to those who consistently give to people in need and bankroll the expenses of our churches. To the faithful pastors and preachers of the Gospel, who proclaim God's Word on the mountain without flinching when the world applies pressure to compromise, know that the time is coming when everything that is done for the Kingdom of God will be revealed and rewarded. Know that The Lord promises us a special crown in 1 Peter 5:4. Some may label us troublemakers, but blind eyes and deaf ears will open to the truth, and people will be saved. Everyone will hear our story, just as we have heard Obadiah's.

We are one body with many parts, but Jesus is the Head. One is not better than the other. We all do things we never thought we could do, and we go places we never thought we would go. In all of our lives, the Holy Spirit comes alongside and says, "atta boy," or "atta girl." Jesus is the Author and Finisher of it all, and our story is actually part of His story.

WHERE THE FIRE BURNS, PEOPLE TURN

I live in the Texas Panhandle, and wildfires are common here, especially when the wind blows, and the wind always blows in Amarillo, Texas. Smoke soars high into the sky and can be seen from miles away. The smell of smoke fills the air, and people always look in the direction of the smoke. Sometimes they look for the source of the fire. Where the fire burns, people turn.

"For our God is a consuming fire." (Hebrews 12:29) The Lord called Moses from a burning bush. He guided Israel with fire in the night. Tongues of fire fell on the believers in the Upper Room. In Revelation, Jesus' eyes burn like fire. The fire of God's wrath will one day fall and consume the earth in judgment. I do not want to experience that fire. I do not want anyone to experience that fire. The good news is that we do not have to. Jesus Christ took upon Himself the fire of God's wrath so that we could experience the fire of God's love.

John the Baptist said that Jesus would baptize with the Holy Spirit and with fire. (Luke 3:16). When we burn with the fire of God, people will turn and look. It is human nature to see what is on fire and to watch things burn. As their attention turns toward us, we can direct them to the Lord Jesus and the welcoming fire of God's love, who wants to save them, draw them in, and burn away the sin in their lives.

1 Kings 18 is one of my favorite chapters because it is my chapter. It is the church's chapter too. If we cannot find Jesus or ourselves in the lives of the men and women we meet in the Bible, then we are just learning a history lesson about someone else. God included their stories because He wanted to show how He works in and through people just like us. Elijah's time upon the earth has come and gone, but his legacy still lives because he built his life upon God's Word. God's story still continues, and it is unfolding in us. It is all about Jesus. It always has been and it always will be, even if the Bible does not mention Him by name. The Word of God points to Jesus. The life of Elijah pointed toward Jesus. Our lives point toward Jesus.

THE TROUBLER OF ISRAEL

"Then it happened, when Ahab saw Elijah, that Ahab said to him, 'Is that you, O troubler of Israel?' And he answered, 'I have not troubled Israel, but you and your father's house have, in that you have forsaken the commandments of the LORD and have followed the Baals. Now therefore, send and gather all Israel to me on Mount Carmel, the four hundred and fifty prophets of Baal, and the four hundred prophets of Asherah, who eat at Jezebel's table.'" (1 Kings 18:17-19)

When Elijah returned to Ahab's court, Israel was in a desperate situation. Drought and famine had ravaged the land, and Ahab should have realized that what Elijah said came true. God tried to warn Ahab, and as each year passed with famine and drought, Ahab should have repented. He should have led Israel to repentance. But Ahab persisted in his rebellion. He either hardened his heart or he chose to continue to walk in darkness. Either way, he hated when Elijah came around because Elijah held God's mirror up to Ahab's face. Ahab did not want to face the truth. The light in Elijah's life exposed the darkness in Ahab's. Ahab failed as the leader of God's people.

Some people will reject the message. They will try to hide from the Word of God. Once or twice a week, someone walks out on my sermons, and when that happens, it does hurt my heart. It is not fun, but I cannot change the message. I cannot change the truth. I cannot make God less than who He is. We are nobody's friend if we do that because people are accountable to God whether they want to be or not.

However, there are some who see and hear the truth, and they receive the message. They embrace it, and a change takes place in their lives. They move from death to life, so we persevere. All we can do is live with the fire of the Holy Spirit in our lives and shine the Light of the Gospel. We remind people that God's love for us burned so hot that He allowed His one and only Son to absorb the fire of His wrath so they could walk in the warmth of God's love.

STANDOFF ON MOUNT CARMEL

"So Ahab sent for all the children of Israel, and gathered the prophets together on Mount Carmel." (1 Kings 18:20)

Sin makes people stupid. There were four hundred and fifty prophets of Baal and four hundred prophets of Asherah. Jehovah had one. Eight hundred and fifty to one. Ahab was so sure that Baal stood a chance against Jehovah that he brought the entire nation of Israel together to watch the showdown. What Ahab failed to realize was that God plus one man or woman willing to stand and do the work of God equals a majority. God used Ahab's ignorance and his arrogance against the enemy. Elijah stood up for God, so God stood by Elijah. It would be no contest, and thanks to Ahab, all of Israel would witness the triumph of Jehovah.

"If God is for us, who can be against us?" (Romans 8:31)

God plus seventeen people started Grace Church in a lock shop. God plus Grace Church built a radio station. God planted both the church and the radio station at the intersection of Western and Plains in Amarillo, Texas. Western and Plains is one of Amarillo's highest points. I call it "Mount Amarillo."

God stood beside us because we stood up for His Word. It was never about me, or our name, or our success. It was always about the people who live in my city. Then it became about the people who listened to the radio or on the internet. People are starving for the truth, and we gave them the Bread of Life. People are dying of thirst, and we brought them Living Water. Everyone is searching for the truth. There is only one Light of the World. We lift Jesus Christ as high as we can. We shine as far as our light can reach. Grace Church is truly a city on a hill.

Mount Carmel was great. Mount Amarillo is great. There is a greater mountain still. Jesus died on Mount Calvary. The Pharisees sought to destroy Jesus. According to Luke 22:3, Satan entered Judas and used him to betray Jesus into their hands. They all thought they had won, but all they did was set up the greatest showdown in history. Jesus told everyone that if He was lifted up from the earth, He would draw all people unto Himself. (John 12:32) All of their scheming simply ensured that the promise would come true.

Calvary was God's plan all along. Jesus crushed the enemy on Mount Calvary. Calvary made Jesus's message stronger and louder, and it made His light shine brighter. His death, burial, and resurrection stripped the enemy of every weapon he possessed. The message of the cross, the message of Mount Calvary, and the message of the Gospel became the power of God unto salvation.

Another mountain is coming, and we will all have the opportunity to witness that event. Jesus will touch down again on the Mount of Olives with His eyes flaming like fire. All of the nations will gather to wage war against the Lord, but He rides through the valley of Jezreel and through the valley of Armageddon. We have the chance to ride with Him. I want to ride with Him. I want everyone to be on His side. That is why I still preach at Grace Church on Mount Amarillo.

MAKE A CHOICE – STOP DANCING AROUND

"If the LORD is God, follow Him; but if Baal, follow him." But the people answered him not a word. (1 Kings 18:21b)

God hates double-mindedness. We either choose the Lord or we choose someone else. Either way, we have to make a decision because lukewarm believers make God sick.

Coming up through high school, I tried to dance with two partners. I went to church to make my mom happy, but at Adams High School I danced like every other teenager in the 1970s. It did not work. The day came when I had to choose, and God settled the matter upside down on my motorcycle. I chose Jesus. He leads, and I follow. The world still tries to pull at me, but the Holy Spirit pulls me back.

We all have to make that choice. Which master will we serve? Trying to dance with two partners who move in such opposite directions will cripple us. Here is my advice. Choose Jesus. The world will use us. The enemy wants to destroy us. Only Jesus wants to save us.

THE SHOWDOWN

"Therefore let them give us two bulls; and let them choose one bull for themselves, cut it in pieces, and lay it on the wood, but put no fire under it; and I will prepare the other bull, and lay it on the wood, but put no fire under it. Then you call on the name of your gods, and I will call on the name of the LORD; and the God who answers by fire, He is God." (1 Kings 18:23-24)

Years ago, Grace Church met at a YWCO. A man named David who had been attending our church walked up to me and said, "Pastor Bill, I love you, but I have to curse you and your house." David belonged to Wicca. I believe in the devil, and when they call on him, stuff can happen. The enemy does have some power, but he is on a leash. He is not equal to God. Not. At. All. God created the devil, and he is subject to God's sovereignty just like every other being in the universe. God created the devil as an angel, but he rebelled against God. He tried to wage war against God, but God kicked him out.

I looked David in the eye, and I challenged him.

"You pray to your god, and I will pray to my God, and may the best God win."

I sounded tough, but I went back to my office and asked myself, "Did I just volunteer my house for a showdown with the devil?" I had a wife and three babies at home. I prayed all night that night, but I also had a seventy-two year old retired pastor in my church named Joe Sneed. He parked his car in front of my house that night and spent the entire night praying for us too.

"Who won, Pastor Bill?"

Twenty-seven years later, Jesus Christ saved David. He died as a believer in 2017, and he is in heaven today. My Jesus won once and for all, and my God is the God who answers by fire!

Every advantage was given to Baal and his followers. There were 850 prophets to God's one prophet. Elijah gave them first dibs over which bull to sacrifice. He would take what was left. Elijah's confidence was not in the crowd, the wood, the bull, or even himself. His confidence was in God, who proved Himself over and over again.

HOPELESS DESPERATION

"So they took the bull which was given them, and they prepared it, and called on the name of Baal from morning even till noon, saying, 'O Baal, hear us!' But there was no voice; no one answered. Then they leaped about the altar which they had made." (1 Kings 18:26)

Baal's response to eight hundred and fifty followers was nothing. They cried louder, and still there was no response: no answer, no hope, no fire. They were devoted, but they were deceived. Their devotion was not the problem. Their god was the problem. There was no reward and no refuge. There was silence, strife, disappointment, and no fire.

"And so it was, at noon, that Elijah mocked them and said, 'Cry aloud, for he is a god; either he is meditating, or he is busy, or he is on a journey, or perhaps he is sleeping and must be awakened.' So they cried aloud, and they cut themselves, as was their custom, with knives and lances, until the blood gushed out on them. And when midday was past, they prophesied until the time of the offering of the evening sacrifice. But there was no voice; no one answered, and no one paid attention." 1 Kings 18:27-29

Elijah had nothing but contempt for Baal. If Baal was a god, why did he not respond? Now was the perfect opportunity to display his might. He was the sky god, after all. How much more would he require of his followers? They were literally spilling their blood to draw his attention. Clinging to this false god only drove them deeper into despair and desperation. There was no hope or rest in sight, only exhaustion and destruction.

That is why God brought Elijah to the top of a mountain. Israel could not see because they were blind. They could not hear because they were deaf. The enemy enslaved them. He exploited them. He deceived them. Their only hope was to see the fire of God fall and hear the Word of God proclaimed.

People devote themselves to all kinds of vain pursuits. Their addictions destroy them. Porn enslaves them. They shoot their god in their arm, drink him from a glass, or wrap their arms around person after person, but their gods fail them and leave them in despair. They think if they get enough likes on Facebook or enough followers on Instagram, someone will hear them crying out. Some even mutilate their flesh because, in some strange way, seeing their own blood gives voice to their pain and desperation.

One fix is not enough. They crave more, and they try harder, but nothing satisfies. The more they strive, the more it destroys them. That is what the enemy does. He is behind all these false "gods," and his purpose is to always steal, kill, and destroy.

It breaks my heart, and I cry for them, but I have nothing but contempt for their gods. That is why I stand week after week at my pulpit in front of my congregation. It is why we broadcast from our radio station. We are filled with the Holy Spirit's fire and shine the light of Jesus. We proclaim His Word because that is the only hope there is. The Gospel of Jesus smashes the yoke of bondage. We do not have to strive. We do not have to cry louder. The Lord hears our prayers. We do not have to try harder because Jesus is our righteousness. We do not have to mutilate ourselves because Jesus allowed Himself to be mutilated for us. He died for us so that we might have eternal and abundant life. He came to set us free!

INVITATION

"Come near to me." (1 Kings 18:30)

Elijah knew he did not need to work up a frenzy. He knew he prayed to the one and only Living God, and God already proved that He heard Elijah's prayers. The rain stopped. The boy was raised to life. Elijah's confidence was not in the words he prayed. It was not in the volume, the length, or the drama of his prayers. His confidence was in the God to whom he prayed.

Elijah wanted to draw Israel close so that they could see. He gave them an invitation, but really, it was the Lord reaching out for them. He wanted to redeem and restore them. He had always been faithful to Israel, even when they were not faithful to Him.

"Come now, and let us reason together," says the LORD, "Though your sins are like scarlet, they shall be white as snow; Though they are red like crimson, They shall be as wool. If you are willing and obedient, you shall eat the good of the land." (Isaiah 1:18-19)

God is still reaching out. Jesus beckoned, "Come to Me, all you who labor and are heavy laden, and I will give you rest. Take My yoke upon you and learn from Me, for I am gentle and lowly in heart, and you will find rest for your souls; for My yoke is easy, and My burden is light." (Matthew 11:28-30)

There is no question about it. If we call out to Jesus, He will respond to our plea. He will save us. If we worship Him, He will inhabit those praises. After I preach, I always give an invitation for people to come. More often than not, at least one person stands, but they are not responding to me. Jesus called them by name. They are coming to Jesus.

RESTORATION

"And he repaired the altar of the LORD that was broken down. And Elijah took twelve stones, according to the number of the tribes of the sons of Jacob, to whom the word of the LORD had come, saying 'Israel shall be your name.' Then with the stones he built an altar in the name of the LORD; and he made a trench around the altar large enough to hold two seahs of seed." (1 Kings 18:30-32)

The nation of Israel began with a promise. God called Abraham, and in Genesis 12, He promised Abraham that if he left everything behind and followed Him, He would give the land to Abraham and his descendants. Abraham responded by building an altar and calling on the name of the Lord. All throughout Abraham's life, he built altars and dedicated them to God.

Jacob was Abraham's grandson. He followed his grandfather's example. He built altars to the Lord.

Altars played a significant role in the lives of God's people. They were memorials of their encounters with God. They were places of consecration and repentance. They were places of worship and thanksgiving. At some point, someone built an altar to the Lord on top of Mount Carmel, but someone else tore it down. The Hebrew word for broken down in this context is harac, which means it was torn down or overthrown. It was not neglected; it was broken. Israel broke their fellowship with the Lord by overthrowing Him from His rightful place as their God, and that altar stood as a monument to the brokenness of God's people.

The first thing Elijah did was repair the altar of the Lord using the twelve stones that represented the twelve tribes of Israel. It was God who had set Israel apart from all other nations. He gave them His name and His Word. They were chosen to represent Him to all the other nations. They were chosen to bring about the Messiah. Israel was meant to be set apart and consecrated for the Glory of the Living God. God's power and glory would once again be on full display as Elijah restored what had been broken and forgotten. The fire would fall and consume the sacrifice on that altar.

God always searches for people through whom He can reveal Himself, and His power will fall upon the man or woman who consecrates themselves to Him. God took the first step. He repaired what was torn down when Adam and Eve sinned in the Garden. Our fellowship with the Lord was broken. He prepared an altar, the cross of Jesus Christ, upon which to place the sacrifice for all of our sins. He provided the sacrifice, His one and only Son. The fire of God's wrath fell upon the altar of the cross. God restored what was broken.

Now, He calls out to us. Come near. He invites us to be living stones from which God will build His temple, which will be centered on Christ Jesus, the Cornerstone. We offer our lives as a sacrifice to Him, and the fire of God consumes us. It consecrates us. It makes us a holy people and royal priesthood through whom God can now reveal Himself to the world as His power and glory are displayed in and through His church.

God did not come to destroy Israel. He came to once again establish Himself as the God of His people. They were hungry, thirsty, desperate, and broken, but God sent Elijah to bring food, water, hope, redemption, and life to His people.

Jesus did not come to condemn the world but to save it through Himself.

"And he put the wood in order, cut the bull in pieces, and laid it on the wood, and said, 'Fill four waterpots with water, and pour it on the burnt sacrifice and on the wood.' Then he said, 'Do it a second time,' and they did it a second time; and he said, 'Do it a third time,' and they did it a third time." (1 Kings 18:33-34)

Elijah took great care in offering his sacrifice, placing everything in order according to God's Word, and then he did something crazy. He commanded people to pour water over the sacrifice. Sometimes God does something so unexpected that the results have no other explanation than that it was the power and the hand of God. Elijah made sure every earthly advantage was given to Baal's servants, but they could have covered their sacrifice in kindling and poured lighter fluid around the trench, but the fire would not fall. Baal was not God.

Elijah already knew nothing could stop God, not even if the sacrifice was dripping with water or if the water ran everywhere. The fire would fall.

"And it came to pass, at the time of the offering of the evening sacrifice, that Elijah the prophet came near and said, 'LORD God of Abraham, Isaac, and Israel, let it be made known this day that You are God in Israel and I am Your servant, and that I have done all these things at Your Word. Hear me, O LORD, Hear me, that this people may know that You are the LORD God, and that You have turned their hearts back to you again.'" (1 Kings 18:36-37)

Elijah did all he could do. He repaired the altar. He prepared the sacrifice. He proclaimed God's Word. He prayed to God. Then, he stepped aside and made room for God's fire to fall.

"Then the fire of the LORD fell and consumed the burnt sacrifice, and the wood and the stones and the dust, and it licked up the water that was in the trench. Now when all the people saw it, they fell on their faces; and they said, 'The LORD, He is God! The LORD, He is God!'" (1 Kings 18:38-39)

Jehovah was God! There was no doubt, no confusion, and no fear of what others might think, say, or do. Everything else fades away when God's glory is displayed among His people. They lifted their voice to their God.

Nothing could stop God. Nothing they did or did not do—not their sin or their rebellion, not the enemy's plans, not even a sacrifice saturated in water—God's fire consumed everything.

Boom! The fire fell!

Boom! It consumed the sacrifice!

Boom! It consumed the wood, the stones, and the dust!

Boom! It licked up every bit of the water!

People walk into my church thinking, "I'm hopeless. I'm so soaked in sin that I shouldn't even be in this building." They drip with it, and it surrounds them. But Jesus paid for all of our sins, every single one of them. He cleansed us from all unrighteousness. He took it all.

"If we confess our sins, He is faithful and just to forgive us our sins and to cleanse us from all unrighteousness." (1 John 1:9)

There is nothing so hard, no sin so great, that it can overcome the power of Christ's blood. Amen!

"And Elijah said to them, 'Seize the prophets of Baal! Do not let one of them escape!' So they seized them; and Elijah brought them down to the Brook Kishon and executed them there." (1 Kings 18:40)

Judgment is real, and it is coming. I cannot talk about the salvation of God without warning us of God's judgment. Christ's whole life and death were about satisfying God's need for a sacrifice so that we could be spared from God's judgment.

How can a loving God also be a God of judgment? Because God is also a holy God. His holiness is as much a part of God's unchanging nature as His love. He simply cannot change who He is. The Good News is that He provided The Way to make us holy, but it must be done in His way and on His terms. Jesus is the only way. To choose any other way is to choose the wrong way, and God will not accept it.

To allow those who preach or teach another way but the true, unaltered Gospel of Jesus Christ cannot be tolerated or allowed a voice among God's people. All other ways end in certain judgment and eternal death.

Here is my counsel. Choose Jesus. Follow Jesus. He is the only way.

BURN, BABY, BURN

I have a chiminea in my backyard, and I cannot wait for the temperature to hit 58 degrees. I go out to my patio, place the wood just so, and light a fire. I love to linger and feel the heat as the fire burns inside. If I sit out there long enough, I will smell like smoke.

On really cold nights, I light a fire in my fireplace and watch it burn. We should all be like that warm and inviting fire in a cold and dark world. People should be able to smell the smoke from the fire that lives inside.

If we strike a match and just throw it in, the fire will go out. We must feed the fire, care for it. We stoke the embers so it can roar back to life.

Remember when God saved us? Remember when all we wanted to do was read the Bible and share everything we learned with the people around us? Over time, we neglect the fire until it is a tiny ember.

The good news is that the ember means there is still fire. There is still hope. The fire has not been snuffed out. Go back to God's Word. Stoke the fire. Spend time with Jesus.

"Did not our heart burn within us while He talked with us on the road, and while He opened the Scriptures to us?" (Luke 24:32)

There is nothing like holy heartburn when I sit alone with God's Word as the Holy Spirit teaches me.

If I ever fall back on old sermons or long for the good ole days, I hope my church finds a new pastor. As long as I hunger for God's Word and as long as my church yearns for the fire of God, we will be exactly where we need to be when we need to be there—a place where people can see the smoke and come inside to see what is burning. As long as the fire continues to burn in us, people will turn. Today is the day. Burn, baby, burn!

THE WORK OF PRAYER

"The effective, fervent prayer of a righteous man avails much." (James 5:16b)

"Then Elijah said to Ahab, 'Go up, eat and drink; for there is a sound of abundance of rain.' So Ahab went up to eat and drink." (1 Kings 18:41-42a)

God saved me when I was sixteen, and I was hungry—starving for God's Word. I spent sixteen years wandering in the wilderness, and when I tasted God's goodness for the first time, I wanted more.

Ahab had just witnessed a mighty display of God's power, maybe for the first time, and he was hungry. It had been a long day, and Elijah knew what Ahab did not.

"Effective fervent" comes from one Greek word, *energeo*, "to work efficiently, and to progress, moving from one stage to the next."

Mature believers know and understand what new believers do not. There is so much more in store, but they are not yet ready. Mature believers know that sometimes we must dig in and do the hard work, not in the flesh, but in the Spirit.

Elijah did exactly what he was supposed to do. He encouraged Ahab to eat and enjoy the Lord, but Elijah knew God wanted to do more. Elijah lingered behind. While everyone else feasted, Elijah fasted and prayed. He entered into the work of prayer, and that is quite possibly the most spiritual and powerful work Elijah did that day. Prayer connects us to the miracle working God, and God did not just promise fire. He promised rain. Elijah would not give up until he saw the rain.

I quickly discovered that ministry is work, and our spiritual gift only functions when we actively engage in the work of the ministry. Our first work is in prayer. Salvation began with a prayer, and at first, we expect everything to be as easy as receiving salvation. However, Jesus' work of salvation cost Him everything.

Israel had been ravaged by the drought and famine, and if it did not rain soon, there would be no food. People would forget about the fire if there was no food. The land needed to be revived. Their souls needed revival.

"Elijah was a man with a nature like ours, and he prayed earnestly that it would not rain; and it did not rain for three years and six months. And he prayed again, and heaven gave rain, and the earth produced its fruit." (James 5:17-18)

Do not get hung up on the phrase "righteous man." No one is righteous, not a single one. However, Jesus Christ imparted His righteousness to us. We cannot do one single work of God in our own power, not even prayer, especially not prayer. We need the power of God, the wisdom of God, and the Spirit of God to pray according to God's will. We all have different Spiritual gifts and callings, but the one calling we all share is the call to pray. We are called to be people of prayer. The church is called to be a house of prayer. God's people pray.

TO SEE AND HEAR WHAT OTHERS DO NOT

I timed Elijah's prayer in 1 Kings 18:36-37. That prayer took roughly thirty seconds from start to finish. God hears our quick prayers. He even heard Peter's millisecond prayer on the Sea of Galilee when he started to sink into the waves. Peter cried, "Lord, save me!" and Jesus did save Peter.

Those kinds of prayers are good, and God responds. But Elijah invested in the work of prayer long before he ever stood atop

Mount Carmel. He spent days, weeks, months, and ultimately years praying with all of his heart for God to hold back the rain.

Elijah was just like us. He had demands and obligations in his life. He had the same twenty-four hour days we have, yet somewhere in his life, he carved out time to seek the face of God, and God revealed to Elijah His heart and His plans. God was going to send rain to Israel. Elijah heard the sound of rain before the first drop ever fell because he had heard the voice of God promise rain.

Elijah could have been satisfied with the fire. He could have stopped there. It was a mighty miracle. The fire established Elijah as a mighty man of God. The fire vindicated Elijah and proved that God heard and answered his prayers. But Elijah's life, his prayers, and his desires were not about himself. It was about the promise of God. God promised rain. It was about the revival and restoration of Israel.

Our lives are not about us anymore. Our lives are about the glory of God. Our lives are about the revival and restoration of the lives of those around us. If all we ever pray are the thirty-second prayers, we will never see the fullness of what God wants to do in and through us.

Many years ago, I started praying for a new work to be done in Grace Church. One day I saw an old grocery store at the intersection of Western and Plains in my city that had just gone up for sale. I pulled over and looked in those windows, and I heard God. I heard the sound of revival rain. I saw the salvation of new hearts and the restoration of old faces. I knew God wanted to do a mighty work there. I saw and heard what no one else did.

I told my congregation, "We're moving!" and I received the same look from the people that I imagined the Israelites gave Elijah when he asked for the last four barrels of water to be poured out on the sacrifice. Many in my congregation thought I was crazy, but I went to work and started praying.

Elijah did not stop praying until the rain fell. I went back into my prayer closet, and I prayed, and prayed, and prayed. I kept praying because I knew my heart and God's heart were in sync.

I still pray for Grace Church, and I will never stop until my time on earth is finished. I also have people in my own personal life to whom I desperately want God to reveal Himself. I carry them into my prayer closet every single day. I pray earnestly and fervently because I know my prayers matter to God.

Each week, dozens of people fill out our prayer cards: people with sickness, families in turmoil, marriages in trouble, people struggling with addiction, and people who need the fire of God and the rain of revival in their lives and hearts. Do we just dump those requests in a big pile on our conference table and lay hands on them and pray in bulk? No! I have seen preachers do this on TV, and I think that it is lame. That is not the kind of prayer that avails much.

My secretaries type them onto prayer sheets and start praying for them as they type. Each Wednesday, my staff prays for them during our staff meeting. Our church-wide prayer group meets on Thursday evenings. They pray too.

Early one Sunday morning, my phone went off at 6:45 a.m. as I was fine-tuning my sermon. It was my friend in California. That would be 4:45 a.m. his time.

He texted me, "Are you up?"

I hit him back, "Yes, what are you doing up? Are you OK?"

Then came the long text with the bad news.

I asked him, "How can I pray?"

Because my friend was so desperate that he was reaching out to me at 4:45 a.m., I immediately entered into fervent prayer to a miracle working God. It is one of the greatest honors bestowed upon a believer when someone reaches out and asks, "Will you pray for me?" Take their cares to heart and pray for them. Is it always a happy time? No! It is work. Is it satisfying? Yes, because it is the work of God.

PERSISTENCE IS KEY

Persistence is a key element to success in any endeavor, and that also applies to praying. Elijah prayed persistently for three and a half years, and the answer was so close. He refused to give up.

Prayer is hard. Distractions surround us and seek to pull us away from our prayer closets, or they prevent us from entering all together. When we fail to see immediate results of our prayers, it plants seeds of discouragement in our hearts, and we abandon our prayer closets too soon.

However, there are people who are tempted by the same distractions and plagued by the same discouragement but who carry the needs and burdens of others in their hearts. They carry them into their prayer closets, where they pray for them by name and refuse to let go until God moves.

There is something special about people who pray like this, not in their righteousness but in their persistence. They know God hears them. They know He truly is the Hope in hopeless situations. They know He is the Answer to the questions that seem to have no answers. He is the all in all, the Source, and they run to Him over and over because they refuse to have their faith shaken by circumstances. That kind of confidence comes only from someone who spends time with God in prayer. They clamp down on His promises like a bulldog, and they refuse to give up. They pray day after day, year after year, and sometimes decade after decade.

SACRIFICE

No one has time for prayer. No one. We all come home from a long day at work or taking care of the children, and then we have the day-to-day responsibilities of caring for our homes and our loved ones. The people of God make time. Sometimes that means skipping lunch, dinner, or even an entire day's worth of meals just so they can have time to pray. They want their prayers to avail much.

Of course, I am going to talk about fasting. Sometimes we say "no" to our stomachs so we can say "yes" to more time for God; more of God's Word, more of God's Spirit, more time before the Lord in prayer.

One of the places I pray the most is in my bed. Oftentimes at night, when I lie in bed and cannot sleep, I talk with the Lord. Sometimes I cry. Sometimes I whisper. Sometimes I do not even say a word, but I always unburden my heart as I rest in His arms. Then I listen to Him.

Elijah just spent the entire day on the mountain, proclaiming the Word and ministering to God's people. If anyone was entitled to rest, it was Elijah. If anyone deserved a good meal, it was Elijah. There was still work to do. God's people needed rain.

While others celebrated and feasted, Elijah sacrificed and fasted. He felt the same exhaustion and pangs of hunger that everyone else did, but the will of God and his desire to see God's Word fulfilled overruled all other human desires.

We are all tired. I know this. We all have crazy schedules. I understand this. Elijah was tired too. He had a long day and an even longer journey to get to this place, but the rain that was coming would revive not only Israel, but Elijah too.

"and he girded up his loins and ran ahead of Ahab" (1 Kings 18:46)

Elijah would outrun a chariot when he witnessed God answer his prayer.

That is the amazing thing about prayer. When the answer comes, when the rain falls, when the victory is won, it is not just the people for whom we prayed that are revived and blessed. Answered prayer gives us the strength and the energy to keep running our race, too.

So keep praying. I have never known anyone to regret a single moment they spent in prayer with the Lord. In fact, I have often heard saints say the only regret they have about following the Lord is that they did not spend more time in prayer.

OUR POSITION IN PRAYER

"And Elijah went up to the top of Mount Carmel; then he bowed down on the ground, and put his face between his knees." (1 Kings 18:42)

Nothing humbles a man or woman of God more than when the power of God falls or the hand of God moves in direct response to his or her prayers. The position of our bodies is secondary to the position of our hearts when we pray, but often our bodies react in response to what God does in our lives. We have seen Him come through in situations we feared were impossible. We are overwhelmed to know that our prayers can actually move the hand and the heart of Almighty God, and we are humbled that the God of the universe would listen to the prayers of an ordinary man or woman.

Elijah did not need a production when he prayed. God had answered his prayers numerous times. Elijah too was overwhelmed and humbled by God, and he was no doubt grateful. However, Elijah was also desperate because he knew Israel needed rain. God promised rain. I believe Elijah bowed in humility and gratitude for what the Lord had already done. He was grateful for the ravens, the widow, and the miracle with the widow's son. He was grateful for the fire.

I also believe Elijah bowed in a desperate desire to see the land of Israel revived by the rain. The rain would bring revival, and God promised the rain. God had done so much already, but Elijah knew there was more.

When my wife and I rolled into Amarillo in 1980, I never imagined all that God would do in and through us. I had no idea what was in store for Grace Church when we started in 1985. We had nothing; no money, no chairs, no building of our own. We prayed for everything.

We needed God to show up, and He did in ways beyond our comprehension. Sometimes, I still feel like the sixteen-year-old kid from Denver, Colorado. I wonder, "How can this be my life?"

I am glad the odds were so stacked against us because the Lord is the only explanation for where we are today. I am grateful and humbled by what the Lord has done. This work continues to grow bigger than anything we ever imagined, and as it grows, so does our need to pray.

Prayer is not our contingency plan. It is the foundation of everything. It was foundational in the building of Grace Church, and it is foundational in sustaining it. We cannot do any of it without God, and that leaves us in a desperate situation. So, when I pray, sometimes I have to bow out of gratitude and desperation because I am so grateful for what He has done, but I know there is more. I need Him to do more, so I bow. Now, at my age, I worry, "How am I going to stand back up?"

I know more is coming. I know it. I know it will be God who does the work. I still pray, and I am acutely aware that I need Him as much today as I did back then. I need the Lord.

EXPECTATION

"and [Elijah] said to his servant, 'Go up now, and look toward the sea.' So he went up and looked and said, 'There is nothing.' And seven times he said, 'Go again.'" (1 Kings 18:43)

I confess that I have sometimes given up too soon on something for which I was praying, especially when it seemed like nothing was happening like I thought it should. What would have happened if Elijah had given up praying for rain after the third or sixth time?

However, Elijah had a history with the Lord. Elijah prayed for years for God to hold back the rain, and God held back the rain.

Elijah knew that to pray for rain was to pray according to God's will and according to God's will the promised rain would come.

Israel's rains often come off the Mediterranean Sea, and the Mediterranean can be seen from Mount Carmel. Elijah kept watching and praying in anticipation that God was going to move.

In Amarillo, Texas, we do not get much rain, so when the weatherman even hints that rain is coming, everyone watches for it. Our rains usually come off the Rocky Mountains, and we all look expectantly to the west on the radar. I knew I heard God's voice about the grocery store, and I started praying. I laid the foundation, not knowing how or when, but I knew Who, and I knew a great work was on the way, so I watched in expectation.

Elijah did not go alone. He had his servant with him, and each time Elijah prayed with expectation, his servant looked in anticipation.

My wife, Cindy, has been with me this whole time, praying, watching, believing, and expecting...just like me. This journey is so much easier when we join together.

Elijah prayed. The servant watched. They both saw the hand of God.

"There is a cloud, as small as a man's hand, rising out of the sea!" (1 Kings 18:44b)

PRAISE GOD IN ALL VICTORIES, SMALL AND GREAT

We prayed for over a year and a half to get inside the old grocery store, and when we finally did, I was not ready for what we discovered...pigeons! Lots and lots of pigeons. They were everywhere, and they left their little presents everywhere. We did not know what we were going to do. We had no money and no feasible ideas on how to get rid of them because there were so many of them.

I met with ten of my guys on a Saturday morning, and we tossed around some lame ideas—a BB gun, a herd of cats—until someone finally had enough sense to say, "Let's pray." So, we prayed.

As we prayed, a man in a pickup truck pulled up, got out, and walked inside. He handed me a business card and said, "I am a professional pigeon catcher, and I have come for your pigeons."

I had no idea that was even a thing!

I asked him, "How do you catch them?"

He said, "With my bare hands."

I asked, "What do you do with them?"

He said, "I sell them to the government. They send them to Iraq to test the air. If they die, they know the air is toxic."

Then, I asked the question I most dreaded to ask. "How much will you charge?"

He said, "Nothing!"

I started to do a happy dance! I knew it was the hand of God that moved. I knew that if God sent the only pigeon catcher I have ever heard of or met at the exact time that we needed a pigeon catcher, that He heard our prayers. Our God can do anything! That was no small victory. That was just the beginning of what would become a place where hundreds, dare I say even thousands, would be saved.

Zechariah wrote, "For who has despised the small things?" (Zechariah 4:10)

"Now it happened in the meantime that the sky became black with clouds and wind, and there was a heavy rain. So Ahab rode away and went to Jezreel. The hand of the LORD came upon Elijah; and he girded up his loins and ran ahead of Ahab to the entrance of Jezreel." (1 Kings 18:45-46)

That small cloud became a heavy rainstorm. God started His church with 120 people who were praying in the Upper Room on the Day of Pentecost.

VICTORY IN JESUS

I pray the fire of the Holy Ghost will engulf the church of Jesus Christ across the world. I pray the reviving rain of the Holy Ghost will saturate the church. I pray it starts at Mount Amarillo at Grace Church.

Our building was once a grocery store—a place to buy bread and water. Now, it contains the Bread of Life and the Living Water. We have had moments with the fire and the rain, but I want more. So many more people need to be saved. I know that is what God wants, so I expect it. Jesus said we need more laborers for the harvest, so I pray for more workers, and I expect it.

Enjoy lunch. Enjoy the Lord, then find a place to pray. It's time to go to work!

Lord, raise us up to serve in the power of the Holy Spirit. Raise us up to stand and declare the Word of God and the Name of the Lord Jesus. Raise us up to do the work of prayer—to pray for our nation and our world. Amen.

Chapter Four

DEPRESSION

UNDER THE BROOM TREE

BROOM TREE

It is easy to think of these men and women as characters in a story rather than people who really lived and walked with God. Consequently, it can be hard to relate to these "legends of the faith".

The name Elijah conjures up images of a strong man with a long beard and strange clothes, standing on top of a mountain, proclaiming the Word of the Lord, and calling down fire.

It is true. He did all of that, but the book of James lets us in on a secret about Elijah. "Elijah was a man with a nature like ours," (James 5:17a) and there was a time when he cowered in fear. He struggled with doubt and depression. He wanted to give up. He was not superhuman. He simply served an amazing God.

1 Kings 18 is the kind of day every preacher dreams of. Elijah stood atop Mount Carmel, declaring God's Word, watching God's fire fall, and witnessing the hearts of God's people repent. He outran a chariot in his victory lap!

God gave us the building! He gave us Radio By Grace! I had the greatest message on earth—the Good News—and I could not wait to declare it to the neighborhood, to my city, to all across the country, and even to different parts of the world. It was more than I knew to even dream of when my wife and I moved into Amarillo, Texas in 1980.

I thought to myself, "This is great! I'm doing what God has called me to do. I'm stepping out in faith, so this shouldn't be too hard! What could go wrong now?"

THE REVENGE OF AN ENEMY

"And Ahab told Jezebel all that Elijah had done, also how he had executed all the prophets with the sword. Then Jezebel sent a messenger to Elijah, saying, 'So let the gods do to me, and more also, if I do not make your life as the life of one of them by tomorrow about this time.'" (1 Kings 19:1-2)

Do not expect everyone to celebrate when the fire falls and the rains come. On top of Mount Carmel, Elijah forgot about his enemy, who waited for him as soon as he came back down: Jezebel. Jezebel was the wicked wife of King Ahab, and she was the one who really held the power in Israel. She refused to give up her hold on Israel without a fight.

Elijah made an enemy in Jezebel from the first day he said, "Yes." to God. The enemy of God placed a target on Elijah's back. When she heard that Elijah destroyed the false prophets of Baal and turned the heart of Israel back to their one true God, her resolve to destroy him only intensified!

I forgot about my enemy, the prince of the power of the air, who opposed God and His people, and as God advanced His Kingdom through Grace Church and Radio By Grace, the enemy strengthened his resolve to take us out.

THE WORDS OF THE ENEMY

Do not underestimate the power of words. Proverbs 18 warns us that "Death and life are in the power of the tongue", with the strength to build up and to tear down. The enemy uses words like bullets from a gun. One word—an angry text or a scathing email—fired off at precisely the right time can inflict wounds that penetrate deeper and do more damage than a thousand lashes with a stick. Physical wounds hurt, but they heal. Hate-filled words wound the heart, soul, and spirit. Words kill our joy, and when joy fades, our strength falters.

Men and women of God must carefully measure the words they speak and the words they listen to, filtering every one of them through the truth of the Word of God. Nothing good comes from listening to the enemy, but if we must listen or reply, put on the whole armor of God first.

Elijah listened to the threats and the lies. This bold, larger-than-life prophet became afraid and discouraged. In his despair, he forgot about the three years that God safely tucked him away. He forgot about God's glorious provision with the ravens and the miracles he witnessed with the widow of Zarephath. He forgot about God's fiery display on Mount Carmel and the refreshing rain showers that revived Israel. Elijah became depressed, and in his desperation, he ran away and hid.

For a brief time, Jezzy got exactly what she wanted. She got rid of the prophet who threatened her plans, her reign, and her kingdom.

I love 1 Kings 19. I love Elijah. I love that God told us the truth about him. He did not always have it together. He did not always stand and fight. He went from experiencing a great, faith-filled victory to being derailed by the words of his enemy. This great ancestor of our faith ran away.

I needed this story because not long after our church purchased our new building and we began climbing the mountain of radio, the enemy took aim and fired with the words I feared the most.

"You're broke. You have no money. You have nothing."

I did not know how to respond. Fear took over, and depression blindsided me like a cheap shot to the stomach. I could not stand, and I could not breathe. The only thing I knew to do was to run from everyone and hide under my desk. Yes! I literally crouched beneath my desk because I did not want to face anyone.

I did not understand it. I had followed God! I knew I did. I dreamed about how God would use Grace Church at Western and Plains to change our city. I expected God to do His thing. I did not expect the fierce opposition, and I certainly did not expect God to seemingly grow silent.

All I heard were the whispers behind my back; people questioning my sanity, my integrity, my ego, and even my faith.

It was hard; hard to read my Bible, hard to pray, and hard to preach to my congregation. I watched in distress as half of my congregation left for "greener pastures." The thought of facing even one more day overwhelmed me. My pride was wounded, my spirit was crushed, and my heart was filled with despair. The joy was gone, and it left me weak. I entered the worst season of depression in my life.

NOTHING HIDDEN IN THE FINE PRINT

"That's not very spiritual, Pastor Bill. We're supposed to live by faith and not by sight."

Maybe it does not sound spiritual, but it is the truth. God never shied from telling us the truth, and Jesus despaired at the thought of what He was about to face on the cross. "My soul is exceedingly sorrowful, even unto death." (Matthew 26:38)

He pressed on, in faithfulness to His purpose, but every step grew more and more painful as the burden of the cross and our sin grew heavier.

The Gospel centers around Jesus Christ! Jesus Christ overcame! Jesus Christ defeated the enemy! Yes! All of this is true, and one day every knee will bow and give Him His due as King of Kings and Lord of Lords, but the first time Jesus came to this earth, He had to suffer. He also warned us that if we really wanted to follow Him, we would have to suffer too. If we want to share in His glory, we have to share in His suffering. It is in black and white. He hid nothing in the fine print.

"In the world you will have tribulation." (John 16:33) Trials, tests, temptations—they are all part of the package, and sometimes they are agonizing. To become the conquering king, Jesus had to first become the Man of Sorrows, enduring the cross to save the people He so deeply loved.

Praise God, it does not end there. "But be of good cheer; I have overcome the world." (John 16:33) He did! He defeated sin, hell, and the grave.

It ends well! I know we know this. It is so easy to say, but sometimes it is difficult to hold onto, especially in the death grip of our worst trials. The ending seems far away, but the pain hurts now!

THE BROOM TREE

"And when he saw that, he arose and ran for his life, and went to Beersheba, which belongs to Judah, and left his servant there. But he himself went a day's journey into the wilderness, and came and sat down under a broom tree. And he prayed that he might die, and said, 'It is enough! Now, LORD, take my life, for I am no better than my fathers!'" (1 Kings 19:3-4)

God was on Elijah's side. The words of a wicked witch could never derail the plans of God, and He was not finished with Elijah, not by a long shot, but somewhere between 1 Kings 17 and 1 Kings 19, Elijah started listening to the wrong voice.

Jezebel threatened, "I'm going to kill you." Elijah prayed, "Take my life now, God."

The enemy masterfully disguises his voice as our own. I internalized what people were saying about me and started telling myself, "You are a fool. You are a failure." The fear of failing leveled me, and I could not even endure my staff meetings. I hid, alone, under my desk. Nothing seemed to work—no Bible verses, no pats on the back.

I hid under my desk. Elijah hid under his broom tree. The enemy did not have to take us out. We took ourselves out, sidelined by fear and discouragement. But there was one thing we both got right. Under the broom tree and under the desk, we both poured out our hearts to God. Deep down, I think we both knew that God still cared for us, so we prayed. The good news is that God was still for us. The enemy was against us, but not God. God is always for His people, and He heard our prayers.

He had already prepared angels to minister to Elijah in his weakened state. God already had men and women in my life ready to minister to my most vulnerable places, and who knows what went on in the unseen realm of the supernatural on my behalf? God always works on behalf of His people—always—through His people, through His angels, and through Himself. I could not see or feel Him then, but looking back now, I see it all so clearly, and I am thankful to the God who hears all of our prayers—our faith-filled shouts of victory and our desperate whispers for help.

TOUCHED BY AN ANGEL

"Then as he lay and slept under a broom tree, suddenly an angel touched him, and said to him, 'Arise and eat.' Then he looked, and there by his head was a cake baked on coals, and a jar of water. So he ate and drank, and lay down again." (1 Kings 19:5-6)

God's plans did not include leaving Elijah to die. God's plans included taking Elijah up in a whirlwind. Elijah would never die, but he did not know that yet. For Elijah to start moving again, he needed healing in his body, soul, and spirit. The Great Physician started by ministering to Elijah's physical body.

Ministering to the physical needs of those who have been derailed, for whatever reason, is as sacred as ministering to their souls. Jesus explained it like this: "For I was hungry and you gave me food; when I was thirsty, you gave me something to drink; when I was naked, you gave me clothes; when I was a stranger, you took me in; when I was sick, you visited me; and when I was locked up, you came to see me." Then we, the righteous, ask, "When did we do this, Lord?" And he will answer, "When you did it to the least of these, you did it to me." (Matthew 25:35-40)

God uses people like angels, and they minister all through my church. When someone finds themselves under a broom tree for whatever reason, they immediately jump into action; running errands, bringing meals, doing housework. It is amazing how much simply caring for the physical needs of those who are temporarily taken out by circumstances can encourage someone to face another day.

Elijah poured out his heart to his God, then laid down to rest. He was too weak to stand. The enemy stole his joy, and Elijah lost his strength. The first angel ministered to Elijah, making sure he had what he needed before he laid down to rest again. One breath at a time, Elijah, and that is an important step when circumstances knock us down. The Lord provides and sustains during those times.

We are the body, that's true, and God uses men and women during key times in a person's life to hang on until the next day.

THE TOUCH OF THE LORD

"And the angel of the LORD came back the second time, and touched him, and said, 'Arise and eat, because the journey is too great for you.'" (1 Kings 19:7)

As Elijah slept, the Bible records another Angel who ministered to him. The "Lord" is capitalized in this verse. Most scholars assert that this was a possible pre-incarnate manifestation of Jesus. This Angel was in a different category. God's faithfulness reaches far beyond our failures, and He does not toss us aside—not when we are weak or discouraged, not when we fail, and not even when we sin. Therefore, we must get back up and start moving again, and we cannot do that with our own strength or willpower.

Praise God for those ministering angels, but that isn't enough. We need the touch of the Lord.

Elijah still had a long way to go, and for him to complete the journey, he needed the touch of the Lord Jesus Himself. Elijah could not pick himself back up, no matter how much he wanted to. Praise God that this Angel of the Lord reached down when Elijah could not reach up and gave him the strength he needed for the rest of the journey to come. God's plans for Elijah did not end with Mount Carmel.

My depression swallowed me whole, and I thought I was drowning. I could not breathe. Not even my wife knew what to do. There was nothing she could do. I needed the Light of Jesus. I needed the personal touch of my Savior. One day the phone rang at the church office, and my secretary answered. She informed the caller, "I'm sorry, but the pastor is hiding under his desk." That day I really was!

On the other end of that phone was my friend Steve Atkins from California, who oversaw radio stations all across the country. He was reading through a list of churches when my name jumped off the page at him.

God instructed him, "Call Bill Gehm." As we spoke, I felt the soothing comfort of the Holy Spirit. Shortly thereafter, my good friend Billy Hobbs from San Antonio called and assured me, "You're not crazy."

I did not know God could sound like Steve Atkins or Billy Hobbs, and I did not know how to pick myself back up—but God did! I could not reach high enough, so God reached down low enough. "He sent from above, He took me; He drew me out of many waters. He delivered me from my strong enemy, from those who hated me, for they were too strong for me." (Psalm 18:16-17)

Jesus still reaches down to us. He did what no one else could do. "For when we were still without strength, in due time Christ died for the ungodly." (Romans 5:6) No one else could rescue us from the pit of sin—not our loved ones, not our religious organizations, not even the angels of heaven. We all needed the hand of the Lord, and He provided for us. Jesus said, "Take, eat; this is My body. Drink from it, all of you. For this is My blood of the new covenant, which is shed for many for the remission of sins." (Matthew 26:26-28) Jesus provides everything we need to revive and sustain us for the long journey, from the depths of sin to our heavenly rest with God the Father. God prepares a table for us in the presence of our enemies. He restores our souls. He leads us and transforms us from glory to glory. He sustains us until we reach Mount Zion, where we will dwell in His house forever.

However, it was not time for Elijah to go to heaven—not yet. Be sure that He who began the good work will finish it! God's plans for Elijah did not end when he came off of Mount Carmel. The touch of Jesus empowered Elijah to stand up and start moving forward again so that He could complete what He wanted to do in Elijah's life.

The touch of Jesus through Steve Atkins and Billy Hobbs gave me strength to stand up and keep moving forward. I still struggled. The battle was not over, but I knew that God had heard my prayers. He still had my back. Elijah could not give up on God because God did not give up on him. I could not give up on God because He did not give up on me.

God remembers that we are human. There is a reason we call it, "amazing grace." But we have this treasure in earthen vessels, that the excellence of the power may be of God and not of us. We are hard-pressed on every side, yet not crushed; we are perplexed, but not in despair; persecuted, but not forsaken; struck down, but not destroyed—always carrying about in the body the dying of the Lord Jesus, that the life of Jesus also may be manifested in our body. For we who live are always delivered to death for Jesus' sake, that the life of Jesus also may be manifested in our mortal flesh." (2 Corinthians 4:7-11)

It was God's idea to partner with these weak vessels! He works through us in the midst of our weaknesses and failures. He uses us in spite of our weaknesses and failures. Sometimes, He uses us because of our weaknesses and failures because He alone receives the glory.

"These things I have spoken to you, that in Me you may have peace. In the world you will have tribulation; but be of good cheer, I have overcome the world." (John 16:33)

Get back up! Start moving! As long as there is breath, there is hope because God is not finished yet!

THE FLAME REKINDLED

The heroes of the Bible were no different from us; and God is still the same God. He reveals His strength in our weakness. He displays His wisdom in our foolishness. I do not know how that works, but it does, and we are able to comfort others because we know the God who comforts us in all of our tribulations.

Perhaps Elijah wishes God would have skipped 1 Kings 19, because, humanly speaking, it was not Elijah's finest hour. I, for one, am glad God did include this season because God used it to comfort me when I found myself under the broom tree. I needed to see the God of all comfort in Elijah's life, and God places people in our own lives who need to experience that same comfort.

The "iron man" of the Old Testament was not the only hero of faith to suffer. The Apostle Paul was the "iron man" of the New Testament. Paul penned two-thirds of the New Testament; he saw the Third Heaven; he was imprisoned for the Gospel, and he wrote these words: "For we do not want you to be ignorant, brethren, of our trouble which came to us in Asia: that we were burdened beyond measure, above strength, so that we despaired even of life. Yes, we had the sentence of death in ourselves, that we should not trust in ourselves but in God who raises the dead, who delivered us from so great a death, and does deliver us; in whom we trust that He will still deliver us, you also helping together in prayer for us, that thanks may be given by many persons on our behalf for the gift granted to us through many." (2 Corinthians 1:8-11)

The Bible uses the Greek word *exaporeo* in this passage, which means to be utterly at a loss, without hope or resources, destitute. Living was too painful, so they trusted in the God who raises the dead. He had delivered them. He was still delivering them. He would continue to deliver them into His hands and care.

Another iron man of the New Testament, John the Baptist, came in the spirit of Elijah to prepare the way for Jesus. He baptized Jesus and literally heard the voice of God the Father say, "This is My Beloved Son in Whom I am well pleased." John saw the truth with his own eyes, heard it with his own ears, touched it with his hands, and proclaimed it with his mouth. However, when he was thrown into prison, he doubted, and he questioned in Matthew 11, *"Are You the Coming One, or do we look for another?"* Jesus simply reminded him, *"The blind see and the lame walk; the lepers are cleansed and the deaf hear; the dead are raised up and the poor have the gospel preached to them."* John did remember, and despite the fear and despair, John followed Jesus to the death. Momentary doubt did not undo his faith. In Luke 7, Jesus himself commended John as the greatest born of a woman.

My point is this. Godly people struggle with depression, despair, doubt, and fear, but God's grace meets us in the midst of those struggles. He met me under the desk just like He met me under the motorcycle. He did not leave me alone to die. He delivered me then, and He delivers me now. I know tough times are ahead, but I also know that same God will deliver me, no matter where I find myself.

THE GREAT PHYSICIAN'S ORDERS – REST

"Then as he lay and slept under a broom tree," (1 Kings 19:5)

Included in God's blueprint for working, is a provision for rest. He worked six days and rested on the seventh. Why did He do that? He is the God who never slumbers, but He built in rest for us. Work six days; rest one day.

Lack of rest leads to burnout. Burnout leads to depression. Depression leads to quitting. I made myself build one day of Sabbath rest into my schedule, one day a week when I rest my body, soul, and mind. My rest is sacred because it is essential to the longevity of my ministry.

I do not have a television in my bedroom, though I do have a ton of books on my nightstand. I want to fill my mind with "God thoughts" that will make their way into my heart as I drift off to sleep. Two metal slats in my bedroom window form a cross. I did not plan on that! In the middle of that window, my wife placed the letters JOY. When I cannot sleep, I look up at that window. I see the cross, and I see JOY. I've created a cave, a hiding place with God. I never want to be under the desk again, and making sure I rest is part of my prescription from God. Rest is holy! God created Sabbath rest for man.

Physical Touch

"Suddenly an angel touched him," (1 Kings 19:5)

There is something special about when the Lord reaches down to touch us. He still does that today. We feel His touch in our lives and in our hearts.

God also uses His church to be His hands and feet. For some people, church is the only place where they can receive that simple "touch" of connection. They do not feel so alone. Part of Elijah's problem was that he felt all alone, and nobody understood.

In the middle of my depression, I attended a Calvary Chapel Pastor's Conference. Those men of God sensed that I needed extra support. Those brothers laid their hands on my shoulder or gave me a quick hug. Some of them prayed over me. That extra connection ministered to my wounded soul as I struggled to leave the desk behind.

I realize the subject of touch is tricky, especially in today's society. Use discernment; whether or not they need a handshake, a quick hug, or a pat on the shoulder. Sometimes, they simply need someone to sit with them. We should use caution and be sensitive to the Holy Spirit's leading, but do not be afraid to establish a physical connection with hurting people. Jesus never shied away from anyone-not the lepers, the diseased, the woman with the issue of blood, or even a dead girl-and His touch always brought healing and restoration.

Slow Down

"So he arose, and ate and drank; and he went in the strength of that food forty days and forty nights as far as Horeb, the mountain of God." (1 Kings 19:8)

The majority of scholars agree that God led Elijah to the same mountain where He spoke with Moses. I do not believe for a second that it was a coincidence. God knew where He was leading Elijah. Mount Horeb was about a fifteen-day journey from the broom tree, so why did it take forty days to get there? Elijah needed to slow down. God raised Elijah back to his feet, and Elijah moved forward, one step at a time, until one step at a time turned into full-on scaling the mountain. Walking with God often looks like that: He leads us step by step and we do not recognize the progress He has made with us until we stop and look around to see how far we have traveled or how high we have climbed.

I take my time in our church services. People "counsel" me that if we trim our services down to one hour, more people would attend. However, I would rather slow down with sheep who are well fed, well cared for, and on pace with God, even if that means I have a smaller church. We still have Wednesday night services so that during the middle of a trying week, we can come together, slow down, catch our breath, and commune with God.

Our relationship with God is more important than the work we do for Him. The work will get done when we are in a relationship with Him because our work is the overflow of our relationship. He breathes in, and we breathe out. The more we commune with God, the less we find ourselves under the broom tree.

GOD'S REHAB

"And there he went into a cave, and spent the night in that place;" (1 Kings 19:9a)

It is amazing how quickly we turn to our own human strength to solve spiritual struggles. We made the mess; now we want to clean it up or hide from it. Adam and Eve did their best to conceal their shame by hiding and covering themselves with garments made from leaves, but these were inadequate for both covering and protection. God stepped in and covered them with the garments He fashioned.

Elijah had his own idea of shelter under the broom tree, but it fell short. It had no protection from the sun or weather, and it had no protection from an enemy who still wanted to kill him. God led Elijah into a cave where He could safely tuck him away with only one way in and one way out. It was likely the same cleft in the rock where Moses hid as God's glory passed by in Exodus 33.

I created my own idea of refuge under my desk, but I was not safely hidden away. My enemy still knew where to find me. I was overwhelmed and didn't want to admit how much I needed help or how inadequate I felt to do this on my own. This life sends some intense storms our way. Our enemy hurls as many fiery darts as he can. We cannot stand on our own. We need the shelter of our Rock, the Rock of Christ Jesus. He is the only way in and the only way out, and our enemies cannot get past Him.

When I am overwhelmed, lead me to the Rock that is higher than I.

"He who dwells in the secret place of the Most High shall abide under the shadow of the Almighty.

I will say of the LORD, 'He is my refuge and my fortress;

My God, in Him I will trust."

(Psalm 91:1-2)

A wonderful Savior is Jesus my Lord, a wonderful Savior to me;

He hideth my soul in the cleft of the rock, where rivers of pleasure I see

He hideth my soul in the cleft of the rock, that shadows a dry, thirsty land; He hideth my life in the depths of His love, And covers me there with His hand, And covers me there with His hand.

(Hymn-He Hideth My Soul)

A HEART-TO-HEART TALK WITH GOD

"And there he went into a cave, and spent the night in that place; and behold, the word of the LORD came to him, and He said to him, 'What are you doing here, Elijah?" So he said, 'I have been very zealous for the Lord God of hosts; for the children of Israel have forsaken Your covenant, torn down Your altars, and killed Your prophets with the sword. I alone am left, and they seek to take my life." (1 Kings 19:9-10)

Life moves fast, and situations can change with the next breath we take or the next phone call we receive. In a matter of hours, Elijah fell from the top of Mount Carmel into the valley of depression. Those things that sideline us-tragedies, our own sin, attacks of the enemy, failing a test of faith- all of those things make it easy to crawl into a hole somewhere and nurse our wounds.

"What are you doing here, Elijah?"

God did not give up on Elijah. No! God made the first move. Elijah needed one-on-one time with God. He invited Elijah into the cave, where He would reveal Himself as well as minister to Elijah's wounded heart. Elijah felt like a failure. He felt like God had let him down and that God no longer cared. He felt abandoned by everyone, especially God.

God wants a two-way conversation with His people. We call it prayer. He desires it so much that He allowed His Son to die, bridging the chasm that separated man from God. He paid a high price for it.

The only way for poisonous roots-doubt, fear, confusion, anger, disappointment, and bitterness (even when directed towards God) to be dug up and removed is to open our hearts to Him in prayer and allow Him access to our deepest spaces.

"Why are you under the desk, Bill?"

I did not yell at God in a cave. I stood in the middle of what would one day be my church's sanctuary, and I yelled, "I did what You said! I am all in, but it is not working! I am losing, my church is losing, and it looks like You are losing! I have been in Your corner since I was sixteen, so where are You now?"

One of the Godliest men I know, one of my best friends, lost his 26-year-old son to a heart attack he suffered while mowing his yard. He admitted to me that he has a hard time praying for his surviving children because he remembers how hard he prayed for his oldest boy. He is a faithful pastor, zealous for the Lord. He prayed, and he prayed in faith, yet his son still died. He still wants to know why.

It is okay to ask, "Why?" Jesus did. Jesus felt forsaken by His Father. He cried out, "My God, my God, why have You forsaken me?" Jesus is the perfect intercessor because he genuinely understands. God remembers we are only human.

God invited Elijah into the cave. He did not kick him out. God did not strike me down in my sanctuary. He met me there. God did not disqualify my friend from the ministry because he struggled with reconciling what he could not understand with what he knew to be true. God remained close and gave him the strength to keep going.

The Good News is that we have an advocate with God the Father.

"For we do not have a High Priest who cannot sympathize with our weaknesses, but was in all points tempted as we are, yet without sin. Let us therefore come boldly to the throne of grace, that we may obtain mercy and find grace to help in time of need."

(Hebrews 4:15-16)

Our High Priest understands because He has been there and overcome. Nothing, and I mean nothing, can separate us from

God's love. We have one-on-one face time with Almighty God because we are tucked away in Christ Jesus.

I descended into the darkness of depression, but the darkness could not overcome the Light of the Gospel. I remember the day God saved me. I remember the countless times God drew me in so He could whisper my name and pour the healing oil of His Spirit over me.

"What are you doing here?"

God never lost sight of Elijah. He does not lose sight of us either. No matter how bad it gets, the Gospel is still the Good News. The Kingdom of God is still coming. Nothing can stop the Word of the Lord. Nothing can stop Jesus, and a mountain is coming that we will never have to leave, Mount Zion. Jesus Christ will be revealed in all of His glory, and I know I will say, "It was worth it." The struggles, the sorrows, the desk... everything is worth it because He is worth it. He is our prize.

A NEW REVELATION

"Then He said, 'Go out, and stand on the mountain before the LORD. And behold, the LORD passed by, and a great and strong wind tore into the mountains and broke the rocks in pieces before the LORD, but the LORD was not in the wind; and after the wind an earthquake, but the LORD was not in the earthquake; and after the earthquake a fire, but the LORD was not in the fire; and after the fire a still small voice." (1 Kings 19:11 12)

Amarillo is one of the windiest cities in the nation. I have seen wind uproot trees, blow off roofs, and even overturn cars, but I have never seen a wind so strong that it can break apart rocks.

God is all-powerful, and sometimes He does things loudly! I like loud. The fire that fell on Mount Carmel was just a tiny peek behind a curtain that conceals a greatness that man can't begin to understand.

People always tell me, "If I could witness one tiny display of God's power, if I could see a miracle, then I would believe." God affirms His greatness everywhere. Romans 1 says we clearly see the invisible attributes of God in creation, and Psalm 19 reveals that the heavens declare the glory of God. The skies proclaim the work of His hands.

Jezebel could see, touch, and smell the rain as it fell around her, but she hardened her heart. Israel witnessed more miracles than any other nation, including miracle after miracle by the Messiah, but it was not enough. They still hardened their hearts. The problem is not with the Lord. It is with our hearts.

The wind, the earthquake, and the fire were manifestations of God's power. They were part of His creation. The gentle whisper was the voice of God; the Word of God. Nothing is more powerful than God's Word, even when it is spoken in a still, small voice. Nothing can stand against God's Word; not winds or earthquakes, certainly not threats from a wicked witch, not even all the forces of hell. The power behind everything is God's Word.

"So it was, when Elijah heard it, that he wrapped his face in his mantle and went out and stood in the entrance of the cave. Suddenly, a voice came to him and said, "What are you doing here, Elijah?" (1 Kings 19:13)

Fires, earthquakes, the ability to break apart rocks and mountains-that was Elijah's God, the One who stood beside him on Mount Carmel. With one snap of His fingers, He could uproot and destroy anything or anyone who stood in His way.

Jezebel could roar and roar. She could even bare her teeth, but God stood beside Elijah. He still had plans for Elijah and Israel, so Jezebel was already defeated.

When God addressed Elijah, God was reaching out to His friend. His voice was as gentle as a soft whisper, but it was filled with the same power that split the rocks. The power was not in the volume of God's voice; it was in the truth of the Words He spoke, verified by the Great I AM.

"Thy will be done."

Jesus turned the voice of surrender and sacrifice into the most powerful force of the ages, with the ability to destroy every work of the enemy and render every weapon of darkness useless. Jesus will return with a shout and a voice so powerful that it will defeat every army that rises up against Him. That day is coming, but it is not here yet.

Right now, Jesus gently calls to us. Come near and find rest for your burdened souls and protection from your fiercest enemies.

I have watched the soft, loving voice of Jesus Christ pierce through the hardest of hearts and bring the toughest of men to their knees. The kindness of God leads to repentance, and when He calls us by name, it changes everything!

"What are you doing here, Elijah?"

God called Elijah by his name. Perhaps Elijah was overwhelmed by God's power, but we know he was overcome by His kindness. He hid his face and drew near to his Friend, his Ever-Present help. The God who brought down fire on His enemies sat with him in his cave of depression as a Friend.

God's glory and man's pride cannot exist in the same space. Elijah yielded his pride, and his heart melted under God's Word, gentle as a whisper. God transformed Elijah's angry, stubborn heart into a humble heart of flesh. A humble heart becomes a soft heart. A soft heart becomes a repentant heart. A repentant heart becomes an open heart. An open heart becomes a transformed heart.

What are you doing under the desk, Bill?

God never lost sight of me. He didn't forget my name. He knows everything about us, including the words we say before we even think of saying them. Sometimes we catch a glimpse of His great power and His great love for us in the same place. It is overwhelming when we understand how much this great God cares about His servants. "Who am I, O LORD GOD? And what is my house, that You have brought me this far?" (2 Samuel 7:18)

Who am I, O Lord, that You would call me by name, that You would choose me, that You would bring me all this way, and that You would be with me until the end of the age?

"And he said, 'I have been very zealous for the LORD God of hosts; because the children of Israel have forsaken Your covenant, torn down Your altars, and killed Your prophets with the sword. I alone am left, and they seek to take my life." (1 Kings 19:14)

Elijah opened his heart, but he still had questions. God listened to Elijah. He communed with Elijah, but God did not explain Himself-not on the mountain, or at the broom tree, or even on

Mount Carmel. He did reveal Himself. He was God. He was sovereign. He was faithful. He was good. Elijah found THE ANSWER. His answer was God, I AM.

Why do the wicked prevail? What is happening to our country? What if they kill us? Could our best days be behind us? We will always have questions, and they will never be answered to our satisfaction if we seek to know the answer with our own wisdom and understanding. The Apostle Peter wrote, "Therefore humble yourselves under the mighty hand of God, that He may exalt you in due time, casting all your care upon Him, for He cares for you." (1 Peter 5:6-7)

There is our answer. We cast all of our worries and all of the things we cannot understand on Him. He cares for us. We will not always understand. We do not have to understand. We have to trust. God revealed Himself in Jesus. Our God saves through Jesus. Jesus is our answer, our wisdom, our understanding, our resurrection, and our life. In Him we live and move and have our being.

THE BIG PICTURE

Elijah felt alone and isolated. We cannot trust our feelings. Sometimes, we cannot even trust our own senses. That is why the Bible instructs us repeatedly to trust in the Lord and not our understanding. Paul reminded us that we walk by faith and not by sight.

Elijah had never been alone. God was with him in every season, and Elijah was not the only one who stood for God.

While God hid Elijah by a brook and provided for him through a Gentile widow, there was another man left behind in the middle of Israel's drought. Obadiah witnessed the massacre of God's prophets. He watched God's people struggle and suffer from the effects of the lingering drought because the king of God's people refused to listen. Obadiah risked everything as he hid one hundred of God's prophets, fifty to a cave, and he provided for all of their needs. Obadiah did not bow. What about those one hundred prophets? They didn't bow either.

There was something Elijah did not know.

"Yet I have reserved seven thousand in Israel, all whose knees have not bowed to Baal, and every mouth that has not kissed him." (1 Kings 19:18)

Elijah could not see the big picture, but God did. Mount Carmel was not the end of the story. It was God's story about God's people. Elijah was a great prophet and an important man, but he was only part of that story. Elijah's call was never just about himself. He understood this from the beginning. Elijah's life was about the Word of God and the people of God, but once he started listening to the enemy's lies and threats, his focus shifted inward. It is dangerous to focus on ourselves. When we look at "Me, Myself, and I," we will run straight back to the broom tree. We were never meant to live for ourselves.

Jesus set His face upward to God His Father, and outward as a servant to His people. Jesus said to find our lives, we must lose them. The enemy will not be able to kill a man who has already died to himself. The enemy cannot steal what we have surrendered and abandoned to the glory of God.

We were never meant to move in our own strength, power, or wisdom. Our weapons are mighty through God. Jesus said in Matthew 28, "I am with you always, even to the end of the age." Amen. Jesus promised that He would send the Holy Spirit, and He would be in us, giving us the power needed to be His witnesses to the whole world. We accomplish God's work by His power according to His Word.

When I crawled out from under my desk, God reminded me of my purpose-my part in His story. My purpose was not to build His church. Jesus builds His church. My purpose was to preach His Word in its entirety, from cover to cover. My purpose was to feed and care for His sheep. That is my place in this beautiful community we call the Body of Christ. It is all about the Lord Jesus. I live to follow the Lord and to obey the Lord. My purpose is to serve and glorify Him. I could not do it alone then, and I cannot do it alone now. The good news is that I do not have to.

BACK TO WORK

"Then the LORD said to him: 'Go, return on your way to the Wilderness of Damascus; and when you arrive, anoint Hazael as king over Syria. Also, you shall anoint Jehu, the son of Nimshi, as king over Israel. And Elisha, the son of Shaphat of Abel Meholah, you shall anoint as prophet in your place." (1 Kings 19:15-16)

A few years ago, my good friends Scott and Beverly Davey celebrated their 50th wedding anniversary. After fifty years together, they can say one thing with certainty: that everything changes. They shed tears of joy in the good times and tears of sorrow when the storm clouds rolled in, but they weathered every season because they built their marriage and their lives on the Rock of Jesus Christ.

Elijah enjoyed the season of miraculous provision at the brook, but that season came to pass. It was time to move on to

Zarephath because God chose a Gentile widow and her son. (1 Kings 17). That season came to pass, too, and it was time to move on to Mount Carmel. Carmel was the culmination of faith and perseverance, and it was a season of victory. However, that season also came to pass as it gave way to the season of testing. The good news was that the season of testing wouldn't last forever either. The season of testing gave way to the season of renewing and restoration.

The cave became a sweet place of refuge where Elijah could hide and commune with God. I know how tempting it is to want to stay in a place that feels safe. It could not have been easy for Elijah to leave the cave behind, but we are not meant to hide away from the world. God is our refuge and our hiding place, but at some point, He strengthens us so He can raise us back up and send us back out.

God's story, our story: it's all about two things-the glory of God and the redemption of His people. God was not finished with Elijah. Mount Carmel was amazing, but that was an old chapter. New and exciting chapters awaited Elijah's future with new mandates and new people along the way. There were new people who needed to hear from God.

Everything changes. It all comes to pass, but hang on because one thing is constant, a fixed point in our ever-changing lives. We anchor our lives in Jesus Christ, the Rock who never moves-our Immovable Mover. In Him we are like the tree planted by rivers of water, whose leaves never wither-a tree that bears fruit in every season to the glory of God.

It was time for me to come up and out from under my desk. It was time to go back to work. The season of hiding was over. He keeps moving forward, but He is the same as he was yesterday, today, and forever, our Ancient of Days. He never changes. He was the same God on Mount Carmel as He was in the cave. God empowered Elijah to stand on the mountain, and God gave him the strength to leave the cave. God gave me the courage to embrace Western and Plains, and God gave me the guts to stand up from behind my desk. It all depended on God. It still depends on God. It will forever depend on God, and that is good because God never fails.

We stand up. We find God's people, and we go back to work.

NEW FRIENDS IN OUR FUTURE

"And Elisha the son of Shaphat of Abel Meholah you shall anoint as prophet in your place." (1 Kings 19:16b)

Nothing is wasted when we surrender everything to the hand of God. It may look like Elijah lost valuable time by sitting under the tree or in the cave, but God used that time. He used it to reveal Himself. He used it to get Elijah's undivided attention. He also used it to unveil some new plans, not only for Elijah but also for a young man named Elisha.

Elijah would take what he learned in the cave and carry it into his future ministry for the remainder of his days. God also used Elijah's story to encourage and motivate me thousands of years later. How's that for a life of meaning?!

It has been twenty years since that season of depression, and I never want to go back under the desk, but I do not want to forget the lessons I learned while I was there. I carry them with me every day into my new beginnings, new chapters, and new friends who await me in the future.

"And he left the oxen and ran after Elijah, and said, "Please let me kiss my father and my mother, and then I will follow you."

And he said to him, "Go back again, for what have I done to you? So Elisha turned back from him, and took a yoke of oxen and slaughtered them and boiled their flesh, using the oxen's equipment, and gave it to the people, and they ate. Then he arose and followed Elijah, and became his servant." (1 Kings 19:20-21)

God gave Elijah a special gift in this young man, Elisha. Elijah knew the cost of following God. He knew the risks, the sacrifices, and the traps, but he also knew the power, the provision, and the victory. God knew that an entire generation of prophets would be trained by Elisha and influenced by Elijah's legacy.

Mentoring someone God has chosen is a great honor, but Elijah wanted to make sure his protege understood what this call meant. "Think about it, Elisha, because once you follow me, there is no going back." There is a great cost to discipleship. Elisha thought about it. He was all in. He gave everything he had in service to those around him, and he abandoned everything else as he followed his master. That kind of zeal becomes contagious, and it renewed Elijah's sense of purpose. We never find Elijah under the broom tree again after he met Elisha, though the attacks did not end. Elijah would face his enemies again, more than once, but this time he did not run. If Elijah had given up, he would never have met Elisha. He would have missed out.

My staff is full of young men and women I would never have met if I'd abandoned my call at Grace Church. I met Todd when he was a kid. He started dating one of the girls in my church, and they endured all kinds of storms, one of which was Todd losing his job. I hired him, and what started out as a job with the radio evolved into a friendship. I baptized him in the Jordan River in Israel.

My young staff-they are all my disciples, polite and faithful servants, just like Elisha, and they are my friends.

THE VALUE OF OLD FRIENDS

The old guys matter too. The young and the old, the new and the experienced, all work together to get the job done. Seventeen people originally started Grace Church, and some of those same friends are still with me. They know the struggles we faced to get to where we are now. They remember me leaving the church between the first and second services on a Sunday morning. I walked all the way to the street corner, and I knew if I took one more step, it would all end. I sat down on a railroad tie, and by God's grace and the unity of friends, I stood up, walked back inside, and preached the second service. To this day, when I want to quit, I drive to that same spot and think about what would have happened if I had taken that step. I do not think about it too long because I do not want to think about what I would have missed out on. I would not know so many people who are now precious members of my congregation. The faithfulness of my old friends, standing alongside me when I was weak, made all the difference.

Get connected. Do not do this alone. We cannot do it alone. God designed us to be part of a covenant community all the way back in the Garden of Eden, when He established the covenant between man and woman. We need each other.

PRACTICAL STEPS FOR AVOIDING THE BROOM TREE

"Rejoice in the Lord always. Again, I will say, rejoice! Let your gentleness be known to all men. The Lord is at hand. Be anxious for nothing, but in everything by prayer and supplication, with thanksgiving, let your requests be made known to God; and the peace of God, which surpasses all understanding, will guard your hearts and minds through Christ Jesus. Finally, brethren, whatever things are true, whatever things are noble, whatever things are just, whatever things are pure, whatever things are lovely, whatever things are of good report, if there is any virtue and if there is anything praiseworthy, meditate on these things. The things which you learned and received and heard and saw in me, these do, and the God of peace will be with you." (Philippians 4:4-9)

Joy in Christ dominates Paul's letter to the Philippian church. It is interesting to note that Paul wrote this letter while he was under house arrest in Rome. It would have been easy to write from a "woe is me" perspective, but Paul found the secret, even when he found himself under a broom tree, so to speak. The joy of the Lord is our strength. He is the ideal mentor for teaching us how to keep our heads above water when sorrows threaten to drown us.

- Rejoice in Jesus. He saved us! Our sins are erased! We're not going to hell! Nothing separates us from God. We will never be alone.

- Let our gentleness be made known. Kindness is contagious. Smile at people. Talk to them. Thank them. Kindness can change the atmosphere in a room. I write "be nice" on my hand every day to remind myself!

- Stop worrying. 80%-90% of the things we worry about never happen. Stop watching the news and open your Bible. Read Matthew 6. The birds and flowers worry about nothing because God takes care of them. It is easy to say, but hard to do. So, how do we do it? Do what the birds do. Sing! Praise God for what He has done. Worship God for who He is. Sing and speak, out loud, the praises of our Savior.

- Pray! The one small word that makes all the difference in a believer's life. Pray about everything, no matter how big or small.

- "Finally, brethren." Become part of the local church. Connect with a church family. We are not made to do the work alone. Not even Jesus walked alone. His disciples were always with Him.

- Filter what enters your mind. There are shows I will not watch, songs I will not listen to, and places I will not go because they will start my heart on the wrong path. Dwell on the good things. As a man thinks in his heart, so is he.

- Follow Godly Leaders. Heed their instructions and imitate their lives.

Paul discovered the secret of lasting joy, and praise God, he shared it with the rest of us.

"For I have learned in whatever state I am, to be content: I know how to be abased, and I know how to abound. Everywhere and in all things, I have learned both to be full and to be hungry, both to abound and to suffer need. I can do all things through Christ who strengthens me." (Philippians 4:11-13, emphasis mine)

TO PRODUCE THE FRAGRANCE OF CHRIST

"Now thanks be to God who always leads us in triumph in Christ, and through us diffuses the fragrance of His knowledge in every place. For we are to God the fragrance of Christ among those who are being saved and among those who are perishing." (2 Corinthians 2:14-15)

People watch us more closely when trials turn up the heat in our lives. Heat enhances the aroma of what truly lies inside, like a pie baking in the oven. People are drawn to what smells good, and when we allow the Holy Spirit to work in our hearts, especially when the heat is dialed up, the fire will not smolder out. Instead, the fragrance of the Holy Spirit will permeate our being and be noticeable to others.

One of my staff would often use an essential oil diffuser in his office, and the fragrance spread everywhere. It never fails: when people walk in, they ask, "What's that smell?" Hopefully, we smell different than the rest of the world when we stand in line at the grocery store, sit in the waiting room at the hospital, or at our work stations. Hopefully someone will ask, "What's that smell?"

We want people to see, hear, taste, touch, and smell Jesus in our lives. I still struggle with depression occasionally, but I know where to run when the heat is turned up. I have found my hiding place in Jesus Christ. I know how to draw near to those under the broom tree and administer the oil of the Holy Spirit because

I have been there. I draw near and allow the Holy Spirit to pour into me, and I watch as He pours out this beautiful fragrance of His presence to all the people with whom I come into contact.

Chapter Five

DETERMINATION

GOD FINISHES WHAT HE BEGINS

THE WORD, THE WORD, THE WORD

I had a little, black-zipper Bible that I carried with me to church when I was a kid, but I set it aside until the next Sunday rolled around. Then God saved me, and I fell in love with my Bible. It became my most treasured possession.

My life revolves around the Word of God. It has been since I was sixteen years old. I made it my life goal to preach every word in the Bible, book by book, chapter by chapter, verse by verse. It took a long time, most of my life, but on October 11, 2015. I accomplished my lifelong ambition when I preached the last word from the Song of Solomon. Now what?

I keep doing what I know God made me to do. People say I should retire; after all, I am in my sixties.

I say to them, "No way!"

I may have only a short time left, but I plan to preach until I die or until I fall off my platform. Maybe I will die falling off my platform while I am preaching. I get dangerously close sometimes, but what a way for a preacher to go!

I ask my congregation all the time, "You have a Bible, but does the Bible have you?"

The Bible is our love letter from God, and it is more than just words written on a page. It is embodied in the person of Jesus Christ. Once we understand this, the Bible begins to talk to us. Sometimes it sings to us. He pats us on the back, kicks us in the pants, yells at us, whispers to us, challenges us, soothes us, but most importantly, He transforms us. He sanctifies us by His Word. The Holy Spirit sits with us when we open the pages, and He reveals a God who loves us. He reveals God's heart, His mind, His will, and His instructions-basically everything we need to follow Him home and to represent Him on the way.

"I charge you therefore before God and the Lord Jesus Christ, who will judge the living and the dead at His appearing and His kingdom: Preach the word! Be ready in season and out of season. Convince, rebuke, exhort, with all longsuffering and teaching. For the time will come when they will not endure sound doctrine, but according to their own desires, because they have itching ears, they will heap up for themselves teachers; and they will turn their ears away from the truth, and be turned aside to fables. But you be watchful in all things, endure afflictions, do the work of an evangelist, fulfill your ministry." (2 Timothy 4:1-5)

Our world seems to be spinning out of control, but it is not. God is still the One who governs everything, and His Word is our foundation. It has not shifted even an inch. It is not hopeless, not if our lives are built on that foundation, and we know that when and if everything falls, crashes, and burns, the Word of God stands because Jesus is alive.

I know many of us hate the word "doctrine", but it is important to establish our lives on true, foundational, and unchanging doctrine because I have lived long enough to witness what I learned intellectually in Bible College and after years of studying and preaching God's Word, progress from intellectual knowledge to experiential knowledge. I have seen those fundamental beliefs of our faith play out in my life, transforming me from the inside out, even now after 50+ years of following the Lord. No one can convince me of what I know to be true. I know it in my head, in my heart, and in my soul because they have been tested and proven.

Yes, I had a season when I questioned the Lord. I had a season when I wanted to cut my losses, hide away, and quit. Sometimes, I have fleeting moments when I still want to quit. But God is faithful. He finishes what He starts in us. Our faith is anchored to the Lord Jesus, and that anchor holds deep and secure, keeping us upright. Jesus holds on tight and does not let go. Our hope is in His Word. Our hope is in Him, so we keep going.

So, what is my plan? I plan to keep on preaching, book by book, chapter by chapter, and verse by verse, until my hope is realized and I see Jesus face to face.

THE COMEBACK

"Go, return on your way to the Wilderness of Damascus; and when you arrive, anoint Hazael as king over Syria. Also, you shall anoint Jehu, the son of Nimshi, as king over Israel.

And Elisha, the son of Shaphat of Abel Meholah, you shall anoint as prophet in your place." (1 Kings 19:15-16)

Elijah may have wanted to give up on the Lord, but the Lord never gave up on Elijah. Sometimes, we think of these men and women of the Old Testament as great tales of old, but they are more than that. Elijah was a real man who had real problems and experienced the same emotions, highs and lows, and ups and downs as the rest of us. God did not write him off. God revived his spirit. He restored his soul. He renewed his passion and determination to finish what God called him to do. Nothing Elijah did was accomplished by his power or strength. Elijah needed God at the brook, the valley, the mountain, and the cave, and Elijah needed God's help to start moving again.

Our failures do not derail God. He does not rip up His plans, toss them in the fire, and wash His hands of us when we let Him down. He does not write us off or forget about us. The only thing He forgets is our sins when we confess them. His grace is greater than ALL of our sin, and it is sufficient. It is enough. We depend on His grace for our salvation. We depend on His grace for our restoration. We depend on His grace for every single step of the journey we take as we follow Him.

The Psalmist said, "And in Your book they were all written, The days fashioned for me, when as yet there were none of them." (Psalm 139:16)

Some of my most powerful sermons and some of my strongest points come from my biggest failures, darkest days, and greatest disappointments. God knew about my darkest days from the moment He called me to follow Him.

The Lord and I have a partnership, but it is the Lord who does the heavy lifting. His strength is truly made perfect in my weakness. What a relief to discover that God's work does not really hinge on me.

What joy to discover that He is faithful when my faith fails. What peace I have in knowing that God's grace is sufficient. It is God's determination to finish what He begins that gives us the strength we need to crawl out from under our desks and get back to work.

"Therefore prophesy and say to them, Thus says the Lord GOD: 'Behold, O My people, I will open your graves and cause you to come up from your graves, and bring you into the land of Israel. Then you shall know that I am the LORD, when I have opened your graves, O My people, and brought you up from your graves. I will put My Spirit in you, and you shall live, and I will place you in your own land. Then you shall know that 1, the LORD, have spoken it and performed it," says the LORD. (Ezekiel 37:12-14)

Most of us never knew a world without the presence of Israel as a sovereign nation, so it is easy to miss the significance of how God fulfilled this prophecy in the 20th century. For almost 2000 years, there was no Israel. It seemed as if there was no way this prophecy could ever come true, until it did on May 14, 1948. God did not write Israel off. Israel is back in the land with their own language, their own culture, and their own religion in fulfillment of the promises written thousands of years ago in the Word of God.

Over 2000 years ago, the Apostles watched Jesus ascend into heaven. The angels told them, "This same Jesus, who was taken up from you into heaven, will so come in like manner as you saw Him go into heaven." (Acts 1:11)

The apostles believed His promise, and so do we. This promise fuels the Church of the Living God today. Between the first prophecy and His first appearing, thousands of years passed. Thousands of years may pass before His second appearing, but we do not get to be lazy. We cannot be discouraged. We cannot stop! Israel is back in the land. Jesus is coming back. His Words are as true today as they were on the first day they were written down. That is why I am more determined than I ever was to finish what God started in me. My life will continue to be about The Word, The Word, The Word.

THE WHOLE TRUTH

Heaven is my home, and I love being an ambassador for Jesus. I do my best to represent Him well. The Good News is that everyone is invited to the table. No group of people is excluded from the gift of eternal life, but that does not mean everyone will receive the gift. Though the gift is free, people do have the freedom to reject it. I cannot make anyone get saved. Oh, how I wish I could, but I can make sure people hear the whole truth before it is too late.

I know what many people think. "I have heard this story for years, Pastor Bill, but nothing has happened for thousands of years." I know they think this because some people flat-out say it to me when they find out I am a preacher.

I warn them not to confuse God's patience with His leniency. I directly benefited from God's patience because if He had come before 1972, I would not have been saved. God does not want anyone to go to hell, and He is still holding the door open.

"The Lord is not slack concerning His promise, as some count slackness, but is longsuffering toward us, not willing that any should perish but that all should come to repentance." (2 Peter 3:9)

In 2 Peter 3:10, Peter warns us that the day of the Lord will come like a thief in the night, in which the heavens will pass away with a great noise and the elements will melt with fervent heat; both the earth and the works that are in it will be burned up.

Judgment was coming for Ahab. He sent Elijah with the warning.

"Behold, I will bring calamity on you. I will take away your posterity, and will cut off from Ahab every male in Israel, both bond and free. I will make your house like the house of Jeroboam the son of Nebat, and like the house of Baasha the son of Ahijah, because of the provocation with which you have provoked Me to anger, and made Israel sin." And concerning Jezebel, the Lord also spoke, saying, the dogs shall eat Jezebel by the wall of Jezreel. The dogs shall eat whoever belongs to Ahab and dies in the city, and the birds of the air shall eat whoever dies in the field." (1 Kings 21:21-24)

The dogs were coming for Ahab, and if he refused to repent, they would rip him apart and eat his flesh. The birds would eat the leftovers. I do not think Elijah wanted to see the king of Israel destroyed. If a warning about certain death and dismemberment did not put the fear of the Lord into Ahab, Elijah did not know what would. Elijah's whole deal had been about the restoration of God's place in the hearts of the people of Israel. Elijah hoped that somehow something he said would finally break through. Elijah told Ahab the truth. Perhaps the fear of total destruction would finally cause Ahab to repent and turn back to the Lord.

The subject of God's judgment is difficult for any man or woman of God to discuss, but it is an important part of the Gospel message. I have preached Revelation four times in my church, and everyone loves the beginning and the end of the book. No one likes chapters 16-17.

"Don't warn people about the birds that eat the flesh in the valley or Armageddon. You might scare some of them away and lose them. Don't talk about hell, Pastor Bill."

I have to warn them because if they listen, God can save them. I love them too much to stay silent, and I do not care if they love me back or not. It is worth the risk if God can use my words to save some of them, so here I am with the warning.

The day of judgment is coming. There will be a day when God will shut the door, and anyone found outside the protection of the blood of Jesus Christ will face the wrath of God. They will be lost. They will go to hell.

Repent. Believe in the Lord Jesus Christ. Call on His name. Today is the day of salvation.

A WICKED STORY

"And it came to pass after these things that Naboth the Jezreelite had a vineyard which was in Jezreel, next to the palace of Ahab, king of Samaria. So Ahab spoke to Naboth, saying, "Give me your vineyard, that I may have it for a vegetable garden, because it is near, next to my house; and for it I will give you a vineyard better than it. Or, if it seems good to you, I will give you its worth in money. But Naboth said to Ahab, "The Lord forbid that I should give the inheritance of my fathers to you! So Ahab went into his house sullen and displeased because of the word which Naboth the Jezreelite had spoken to him; for he had said, "I will not give you the inheritance of my fathers. And he lay down on his bed, and turned away his face, and would eat no food. But Jezebel, his wife, came to him, and said to him, "Why is your spirit so sullen that you eat no food?" He said to her, Because I spoke to Naboth the Jezreelite, and said to him, 'Give me your vineyard for money; or else, if it pleases you, I will give you another vineyard for it. "And he answered, 'I will not give you my vineyard." (1 Kings 21:1-6)

Ahab had the entire kingdom of Israel at his disposal, so why did he insist on taking Naboth's vineyard? Ahab held the position of king of Israel, and he could have enjoyed the blessings of God that came with being the leader of God's people. But Ahab threw it all away when he decided he would rather please his wife than the Lord. He would rather honor her wishes and worship an idol than honor the true God of Israel.

Naboth, on the other hand, knew the value of his vineyard. It was his family's inheritance, and a blessing from the Lord. It meant everything to him, and nothing Ahab offered could convince him to trade his precious heritage.

Ahab could not understand that kind of thinking because he was so far removed from the person God intended for the kings of His people to be. As king of God's people, he was called to serve first God, and then His people. There were lots of other places where Ahab could have planted his tomatoes, but he was fixated on the one plot of land he could not have. It sounds awfully similar to another couple in the Garden of Eden.

I could not find a better illustration of coveting than Ahab's actions against Naboth.

Instead of focusing on what Ahab did have, he could only see the one thing that Naboth had that he did not. Jealousy and resentment against this man grew, and pretty soon it consumed him.

There may be more of Ahab in me than I care to admit. There have been times when I pouted at the Lord like a spoiled child. I pouted because I could not drive the car that I wanted. Is it not enough that He gave me the keys to the kingdom? When I really hear myself, it makes me want to repent. The Lord has blessed me with everything. Am I really going to focus on the one thing I think I need but do not have?

Entitlement does not reflect the character of the Lord. Humility does. The entire life and ministry of Jesus Christ was about letting go of His entitlement to serve, save, and restore.

We must be careful when we find those kinds of thoughts beginning to take root in our hearts and minds because when we start to focus on what those around us have, we start thinking, "What I have is not enough." We start to want what they have, and jealousy and resentment can begin to consume us.

"Then Jezebel, his wife, said to him, you now exercise authority over Israel! Arise, eat food, and let your heart be cheerful; I will give you the vineyard of Naboth the Jezreelite." (1 Kings 21:7)

Bitterness spreads and poisons everything. Ahab was bitter because Naboth would not give him what he wanted. Jezebel was bitter because she thought that it was their right as king and queen of Israel to just be able to take what they wanted. They devised an evil plot against Naboth.

"And she wrote letters in Ahab's name, sealed them with his seal, and sent the letters to the elders and the nobles who were dwelling in the city with Naboth." (1 Kings 21:8)

"So the men of his city, the elders and nobles who were inhabitants, did as Jezebel had sent to them, as it was written in the letters which she had sent to them. They proclaimed a fast, and seated Naboth with high honor among the people. And two men, scoundrels, came in and sat before him; and the scoundrels witnessed against him, against Naboth, in the presence of the people, saying, 'Naboth has blasphemed God and the king." Then they took him outside the city and stoned him with stones, so that he died. Then they sent to Jezebel, saying, "Naboth has been stoned and is dead." (1 Kings 21:11-14)

See how destructive envy, jealousy, and bitterness can be. Naboth did nothing wrong. He was honoring his family. He was honoring the Lord. He simply wanted to preserve what the Lord had given him, and the leader of God's people resented him for it. Ahab tricked Naboth and used the sacred act of fasting to lure him to his destruction. Ahab and Jezebel spread lies about Naboth and used God's name to get away with assassinating him. It was a blasphemous and profane act against an innocent man of God.

ELIJAH: FRIEND OR FOE?

When Jezebel heard the news, she said to Ahab, "You know the vineyard Naboth wouldn't sell you? Well, you can have it now! He's dead." So Ahab immediately went down to the vineyard of Naboth to claim it.

If this story ended here, I would be mad! Where was the Lord?

Sometimes, it does look like the bad guys' win, and we ask God, "Did I keep my heart pure for nothing? Did I keep myself innocent for no reason?"

Ahab and Jezzy may look like they had everything they wanted, but they were not fine. The Lord saw everything, and this wicked scheme would not go unnoticed by God. Technically, Ahab and Jezzy could have blamed Naboth's death on the scoundrels. They could point the finger at the men who stoned Naboth. They were the ones who killed him. But they could not hide their guilt from God, and judgment was coming.

No one is getting away with wickedness-not the politicians, not the corrupt religious leaders, not the corrupt business leaders, not ourselves. No one! God keeps accurate records. No one can outrun God. No one can hide from Him. We cannot deflect our guilt onto someone or something else, and judgment is coming unless we heed the warning and repent.

HEED THE WARNING

"Arise, go down to meet Ahab, king of Israel, who lives in Samaria. There he is, in the vineyard of Naboth, where he has gone down to take possession of it. You shall speak to him, saying. Thus says the Lord: "In the place where dogs licked the blood of Naboth, dogs shall lick your blood, even yours." (1 Kings 21:18-19b)

God is slow to anger and quick to forgive. He does and will punish sin, but He is not eager to do so. He sent Elijah ahead with the warning. Ahab saw Elijah as his enemy.

"Have you found me, O my enemy?" (1 Kings 21:20b)

Ahab had no better friend than Elijah, who consistently told him the truth despite the risk to himself. Ahab was not fine. His destruction was quickly approaching. This would be the last conversation Elijah would have with Ahab, and he did not waste time or words. Elijah did not lose confidence in God's Word or its power to transform death and despair into hope and new life, but Elijah could not make the king of Israel listen. Elijah did everything he was supposed to.

"And he answered, I have found you, because you have sold yourself to do evil in the sight of the Lord; Behold, I will bring calamity on you, I will take away your posterity, and will cut off from Ahab every male in Israel, both bond and free." (1 Kings 21:21)

When I preach my sermons, I never know if these may be the last words someone in my congregation hears from me. I may see them on Sunday, and then by Wednesday night, they might be killed in a car wreck or die from a sudden heart attack. Eternity is one breath away. If we see people with that perspective, it will change everything about the way we interact with them. We would not be concerned about whether they reject us as long as they accept the message that we bring.

I do not enjoy preaching about hell. I never look forward to the portion of Revelation about the flesh-eating birds, but I thank God for warning us in His Word so that we are not left behind to endure that day. We do not have to end up in hell.

The day of reckoning is coming for everyone. For some, it will be a day of celebration as we receive the long-awaited commendation from Jesus, "Well done, my good and faithful servant." For others, it will be a day of mourning as the Lord turns them away. "Depart from Me, you cursed, into the everlasting fire prepared for the devil and his angels:"

Everyone thinks they are fine, doing their own thing, going their own way-that is, until the man or woman of God reminds us of what God's Word says.

Have you ever lusted after someone? Busted! You are an adulterer.

Have you ever hated someone? Busted! You are a murderer.

Those are not my words. They are the words of Jesus. People either try to hide from the preacher or go to the other extreme and get in my face. They think I am picking on them. They think I am their enemy. They think that I am coming for them.

I am coming after them in a way because they do not understand how much I care about their soul. Even if they never open the Bible again or listen to another sermon by Pastor Bill, they are still held accountable to the Word of God. I understand their reluctance and their frustration. No one can live up to those standards.

1 could not either. No one can. The Good News is that we do not have to because Jesus already did. He washes away our sin, and we can start over as if we had never sinned.

We all need a Savior. I believe so strongly in the power of the Gospel because I know its power firsthand. I am a chief sinner, saved by the grace of God. Whosoever may come. Anyone can be saved. All we have to do is ask.

As long as there is breath, there is hope. Way back in the day, when I attended Bible College, my cousin, Peter D., lived like the devil. He ran with the gangs. He stole. He was so bad that when he went to trial, the judge gave him a choice between Vietnam and prison. Peter chose Vietnam, and when he came back, he was crazy. I used to think Peter D. had the one heart that was too hard to yield. I was wrong.

Was there any hope for Peter D. or for Ahab? There certainly would not be unless someone was willing to risk everything to warn them of God's judgment and tell them the Good news of God's grace and mercy.

A CALL FOR REPENTANCE

"So it was, when Ahab heard those words, that he tore his clothes and put sackcloth on his body, and fasted and lay in sackcloth, and went about mourning." (1 Kings 21:27)

When God sends a warning, it is because He wants to save people from destruction. If God exposes sin, it is because he wants people to repent. God does not want anyone to perish. If He did, He would never have allowed Jesus to suffer the way He suffered. He wants restoration. He wants reconciliation.

Ahab repented; true, sincere, heartfelt repentance. We know it was sincere because it moved the heart of God.

"See how Ahab has humbled himself before Me? Because He has humbled Himself before Me, I will not bring the calamity in his days. In the days of his son I will bring the calamity on his house." (1 Kings 21:29)

Way to go, Ahab!

No one is out of reach for the Savior. Jesus went down to the lowest depths, and He ascended to the highest heights, and His blood reaches high and low for anyone who repents. I wrote Peter D. off, but God did not. Peter D. humbled himself, and God saved him. It was not a one-time, "walk down the aisle, get out of hell free" kind of decision. Once Peter made up his mind, he dove all the way into the deep end. He even became a deacon in his church.

THERE IS A REASON WE CALL IT AMAZING GRACE

Not many people "amen-ed" this part of the story when I preached it to my congregation. Ahab repented. Great, but what about Naboth? Naboth was still dead. As far as we knew at this point, he still had Naboth's vineyard. Ahab deserved to die, but at the very least, did he not deserve to pay some kind of penalty for what he did?

Do not worry about Naboth. Naboth is fine. He is in heaven.

The truth is, we are all murderers, thieves, liars, and scoundrels. God's Word exposes the truth, not to destroy us, but to save us. The temple elders in Jerusalem, the nobles, and the priests-they all plotted to kill Jesus. The crowd turned against Him and mocked Him. Jesus absorbed God's wrath and faced God's judgment for our sin, and not only do we not get the punishment we deserve, but we are given eternal life and sonship with God the Father in its place. Salvation was not fair. Grace and mercy are not fair. None of that was fair to Jesus, who lived a perfect and blameless life, when He died in my place on the cross. Our sin was imputed to Jesus, and His righteousness is credited to us.

All we do is say "Yes" and "Amen."

Jesus made it fair by settling our debt.

If we reject that deal, if we refuse to humble ourselves and submit to the Lordship of Jesus Christ, we will face judgment. However, for now, God still delays that judgment and sends prophets, preachers, friends, Sunday School teachers, and

Children's Church workers so that we can hear the message one more time.

"How then shall they call on Him in whom they have not believed? And how shall they believe in Him of whom they have not heard? And how shall they hear without a preacher?"

(Romans 10:14)

For sixteen years, God sent messengers my way with the truth. My mother, VBS workers, Children's Church workers, and Sunday School teachers all told me the truth, but I hated church. I was a thief. I hated people, and I cursed them. That made me a murderer. In his mercy, God delayed my judgment and gave me one more chance when I came face to face with my own destruction upside down on my motorcycle.

I was bogged down by the weight of my sin, but the moment I bowed my knees and repented, righteousness, grace, and mercy replaced hopelessness, guilt, and shame. I felt the weight of sin lift from my shoulders, and I knew the old Bill died the moment I stood up and walked away from the wreckage. A new man stood in his place, and I have never looked back. I knew I should have died that day, and I knew it was not fair. However, I recognized the gracious opportunity that had been given to me, and I was not going to blow it this time. This time, I got it right. I humbled myself, repented, and God lifted me up.

We have people in our lives, like Ahab and Peter D., whom we fear will never listen to the truth. They will never humble themselves. Do not stop loving them. Do not stop praying for them. Keep reaching out. Keep speaking up. They may not listen. They may reject us and tell us to get lost. They may hurt our feelings, but who cares? The stakes are too high, and there are many things more important than our feelings, such as the souls of people.

Maybe if we try even just one more time, it will stick. It could be their moment of salvation. They might repent and become like Paul the Apostle, the self-proclaimed chief of sinners, who became one of the driving forces in the early church. God can save anyone.

THE TRAGIC ENDING

Ahab could have had one of the greatest stories of all of Israel's kings: a wicked king transformed by the grace and mercy of God into one of Israel's great leaders. God revealed Himself in an unmistakable way to Ahab on Mount Carmel. He sent prophets when Ahab went off track. He sent Elijah to warn him that judgment was coming. Ahab could not blame his sin on a lack of knowledge or revelation. He had so many chances to make the right choice, but Ahab chose himself every time.

I have said from the beginning that I see much of myself in Elijah, in both his strengths and his weaknesses. I hate to admit it, but sometimes I see myself in Ahab, too. I sometimes choose my will over God, and it is not from a lack of God's presence or His Word in my life. God has been in my life since 1972, and His Word is my job. Sometimes, I just want my own way.

Ahab, Elijah, and I all inherited the same sin nature, and none of us is immune to its trappings. But we can choose which way to go. We can lean into our own understanding, follow our hearts and desires, and do whatever makes us happy. That is what everyone says to do, right?

"Live your truth. Go your own way."

They are wrong. There is only one way to go and one truth to follow. It is not a bad thing to yield ourselves to the Lord. In fact, we will look like Jesus more than ever when we choose God's will over our own desires. We reflect Jesus when we lay down what we want in favor of others or what is good for them.

Israel was a wreck because the kings kept living for themselves, and Ahab was the worst. Our ways lead to destruction, and not just in our own lives. Living for ourselves destroys marriages, families, businesses, churches, and even entire nations. Our way is the wrong way.

So what do we do? We want to do the right thing. We want to yield our lives to the Lordship of God, but how?

The Good News is that we have a Savior, and He overcame. In the Garden of Gethsemane, Jesus wrestled with the very human desire to avoid pain and suffering as well as his desire to do God's will. At any point, He would have been completely justified in saying, "This is too much for me, and they won't even fully appreciate what I am about to do for them."

But He did not do that. He chose the will of God, which was to kill Him so that we could live. He chose us because His death was the only way we could live. But guess what?! Jesus did not stay dead. He rose from the dead, and He overcame.

Because He overcame, we can overcome too. The life we now live; we live by faith in the Son of God. It is not by might nor by power, but it is all by the Spirit of the Lord. That is God's plan for us: to depend on Him for everything and not just our initial salvation but also for every step we take thereafter.

Elijah needed God's power to climb out of the cave. I needed God's power to climb out from under my desk. I need God's power to take my next breath. Ahab saw the fire fall. He saw the rain fall. Ahab could have reached out to God for help to be a good king and do the right thing, not just for himself but also for Israel. However, he did not, and his choice led to his own destruction.

This does not have to be our story. We could look like Elijah instead of Ahab, and even on those days when we failed so miserably that we could not face ourselves in the mirror, we listened to the Lord. We allow Him to renew and restore, get up, and start going the right way.

"Now, three years have passed without war between Syria and Israel. Then it came to pass, in the third year, that Jehoshaphat, the king of Judah, went down to visit the king of Israel. And the king of Israel said to his servants, 'Do you know that Ramoth in Gilead is ours, but we hesitate to take it out of the hand of the king of Syria?" So he said to Jehoshaphat, 'Will you go with me to fight at Ramoth Gilead? Jehoshaphat said to the king of Israel, 'I am as you are, my people as your people, my horses as your horses. Also, Jehoshaphat said to the king of Israel, 'Please inquire for a word of the Lord today." (1 Kings 22:1-5)

While Ahab earned the distinction of being Israel's most wicked king, there was another king of God's people. His name was King Jehoshaphat, and he was the king of Judah. He had the reputation of being Judah's reformer who followed God. Ahab and Jehoshaphat were connected by marriage. Ahab's daughter married Jehoshaphat's son. They were in-laws.

It was Ahab's idea to attack Syria, but it never even crossed his mind to consult the Lord. Jehoshaphat got it. He knew not to make a move involving God's people without first consulting the Lord. These two kings had completely different approaches to how they ruled God's people.

"Then the king of Israel gathered the prophets together, about four hundred men, and said to them, 'Shall I go against Ramoth Gilead to fight, or shall I refrain? So they said, 'Go up, for the Lord will deliver it into the hand of the king.' And Jehoshaphat said, 'Is there not still a prophet of the LORD here, that we may inquire of Him?' (1 Kings 22:6-7)

The four hundred prophets told Ahab what he wanted to hear, but Jehoshaphat did not trust them. He had good reason not to trust them. If they were truly God's prophets, then why was Israel in such a mess? Why did idol worship abound in Israel? These were not men of God. They did not serve the Lord. They served themselves, and they traded the truth of God's Word for position and influence with the king. Was there no one left in the land who valued the Word of God over the popular opinion of the day? Was there no one left to speak the truth?

"So the king of Israel said to Jehoshaphat, 'There is still one man, Micaiah, the son of Imlah, by whom we may inquire of the Lord; but I hate him, because he does not prophesy anything good concerning me, but evil." And Jehoshaphat said, 'Let not the king say such things! 1 Kings 22:8

Do not despise the Word of God, Ahab. Do not despise the Word of God, saint of God, especially when God seeks to correct us. God corrects those He loves. He wants to steer us to the right path, the path of life everlasting. We cannot grow into the man or woman God wants us to be if we reject the parts of the Bible that challenge or convict us. But, I promise, when we submit to the Word's authority in our lives, we will never regret it. We will always regret the times we chose to ignore it, as Ahab would soon find out.

"Then the messenger who had gone to call Michaiah spoke to him, saying, 'Now listen, the words of the prophets with one accord encourage the king. Please, let your word be like the word of one of them, and speak encouragement.' And Micaiah said, 'As the LORD lives, whatever the LORD says to me, that will I speak." (1 Kings 22:13-14)

Paul warned Timothy in his second letter that a time would come when no one would want to hear the truth anymore. They would not love God. They would love themselves and whatever made them happy, finding preachers who would tell them whatever they wanted to hear. Those preachers and teachers do not care about the souls of the people to whom they minister any more than the false prophets cared about Israel or the people of Israel. They care about keeping their status, their position, and their political influence. I might even be tempted to go so far as to say they do not care about God. If they did, they would approach God's Word with fear and trembling because every word they speak in "His name" and by "His authority" will be evaluated by Him, face to face. They will be called to the carpet for what they preached, for what they taught.

There is actually a special blessing for those who preach the Word with integrity, rightly divided, in its context. God honors those who pore over the text and try to extract the truth of what God is saying and how that applies to our lives. It is a holy calling, and God takes His Word seriously. He admonished Timothy to keep on preaching the truth. Woe be to men or women of God who pretend to speak in the name of God simply to gain favor and position with the people around them! Lies and half-truths will not save you.

Michaiah would only say what the Lord told Him to say-nothing more and nothing less. Way to go, Michaiah.

"Therefore, look! The Lord has put a lying spirit in the mouth of all these prophets of yours, and the Lord has declared disaster against you." (1 Kings 22:23)

Micaiah told Ahab the truth about what was going to happen. Not only that, but he revealed the lies the other prophets told him and the source from which they spoke. Listening to them would bring certain death. God tried to warn Ahab one more time, but Ahab always listened to the wrong voices, even when Jehoshaphat told him they were the wrong voices.

Ahab hardened his heart for the last time. God's patience ran out. Time was up, and Ahab used up his last chance.

JUDGMENT IS HERE

"So the king of Israel and Jehoshaphat, the king of Judah, went up to Ramoth Gilead. And the king of Israel said to Jehoshaphat. 'I will disguise myself and go into battle, but you put on your robes. So the king of Israel disguised himself and went into battle." (1 Kings 22:29-30)

No one can hide from God. No one can escape Him. We cannot throw a hoodie on and think that God will not recognize us! He sees everything we are doing, everywhere we are going, and even every thought that we are thinking. And if that is not scary enough, one day we will see Him face to face and give an account for everything we did. The Good News is that if we are in Jesus and if we listen to the right voice, we do not have to fear that day. That day will not be a day of destruction. However, without Jesus, it will be, and there is no escaping God's judgment once our window of grace closes.

"Now a certain man drew a bow at random, and struck the king of Israel between the joints of armor." (1 Kings 22:34)

Ahab's window of grace had closed. The soldier may have drawn at random, but God took aim, and He guided that arrow in fulfillment of His Word.

Ahab tried to outsmart God. He could not. He tried to run from God. He could not run far enough. He tried to hide from God. It did not work. God knew exactly where to send the arrow.

What a sad ending for the king of Israel.

"So I will make the house of Ahab like the house of Jeroboam the son of Nebat, and like the house of Baasha the son of Ahijah. The dogs shall eat Jezebel on the plot of ground at Jezreel, and there shall be none to bury her." (2 Kings 9:9-10)

Jezebel did not get away with anything either. God did not forget about the prophets she murdered. He did not forget about Naboth. God appointed a man named Jehu to carry out his vengeance against this wicked witch of Israel, and he wasted no time in carrying out his purpose.

"Then he said, "Throw her down." So they threw her down, and some of her blood spattered on the wall and on the horses; and he trampled her underfoot. And when he had gone in, he ate and drank. Then he said, "Go now, see to this accursed woman, and bury her, for she was a king's daughter. So they went to bury her, but they found no more of her than the skull and the feet and the palms of her hands. Therefore, they came back and told him. And he said, "This is the word of the LORD, which He spoke by His servant Elijah the Tishbite, saying, "On the plot of ground at Jezreel dogs shall eat the flesh of Jezebel; and the corpse of Jezebel shall be as refuse on the surface of the field, in the plot at Jezreel, so that they shall not say, 'Here lies Jezebel.''' (2 Kings 9:33-37)

God's Word came true, just like Elijah predicted, and though it seemed like God was delaying His judgment, once the appointed time had come, the judgment came swiftly and decisively. The dogs came, and there was nothing left. She was gone forever. Nothing. No grave or memorial.

"For the word of God is living and powerful, and sharper than any two-edged sword, piercing even to the division of soul and spirit, and of joints and marrow, and is a discerner of the thoughts and intents of the heart." (Hebrews 4:12)

God's arrow knew where to strike Ahab, and His Word knows exactly where to pierce us, but His aim is not to wound or kill us. It is to save us. It may seem like the Lord is delaying His coming, but rest assured, He is coming, and when the appointed time comes, it will be swift and sudden, like a thief in the night.

JEZZY, THE MOLE

Jezebel did not destroy Israel from the outside. Someone let her in, and the rest of Israel tolerated her presence. Maybe it was out of fear or intimidation, or maybe they preferred her god, a god made in man's image who appealed to their fleshly nature and desire for convenience.

"Nevertheless, I have a few things against you, because you allow that woman, Jezebel, who calls herself a prophetess, to teach and seduce My servants to commit sexual immorality and eat things sacrificed to idols. And I gave her time to repent of her sexual immorality, and she did not repent. Indeed, I will cast her onto a sickbed, and those who commit adultery with her into great tribulation, unless they repent of their deeds."

(Revelation 2:20-23)

Jezebel's spirit still lives. God cares about the sexual lives of His people, and it is scary how quickly seductive lies can work their way into the Body of Christ and wreck everything. Anything that crosses the boundaries of the Biblical marriage bed is sin. We cannot honor God in our sexual lives without God's Word in its full counsel. We cannot do it without the Spirit of God having free rein over our sexual thoughts and deeds.

I try my best to preach the whole counsel in its context, centering the truth, God's love, grace, and mercy in each sermon. I expect it from anyone who preaches from my pulpit and from anyone who preaches on Radio by Grace.

Elijah kept preaching for the sake of anyone who would listen and be saved. Grace and mercy were at the heart of his whole deal, but neither Jezzy nor Ahab listened. They pushed God out. God tried to get back in more than once, but they rejected God and reaped the consequences of their choice.

I have Good News. There is still time! Jesus absorbed God's wrath and judgment so that we could receive grace, mercy, and salvation. Jesus stands at the door of our hearts and our churches.

"Behold, I stand at the door and knock. If anyone hears My voice and opens the door, I will come in to him and dine with him, and he with Me." (Revelation 3:20)

Jesus wants to dine with us. He wants to fellowship with us. Listen to His voice alone, and not anyone else's. Let. Him. In. Amen.

MAN ON FIRE

Ahab and Jezebel were gone, and their son, Ahaziah, took his father's place as king of Israel. They did not leave much of a foundation on which Ahaziah could build his reign, and sadly, he followed in the footsteps of his father.

Our kids are watching us. Do our actions at home match what we do and say at church?

What is our relationship to the Word of God? How do we handle adversity? How do we treat other people?

It only takes one generation to upend the groundwork laid down by past generations.

After Solomon's death, each king after him drifted further and further from God's Word until Israel was almost unrecognizable.

On the other hand, it just takes one generation to say, "I'm going to follow the Lord. I am going to obey His Word." One person can change the direction of an entire family.

Paul had no biological children, but he had a son in the faith, and he poured himself into Timothy. But long before Paul came into Timothy's life, his Godly mother and grandmother laid the foundation of faith in God's Word.

"When I call to remembrance the genuine faith that is in you, which dwelt first in your grandmother Lois and your mother Eunice, and I am persuaded is in you also." (2 Timothy 1:5)

Paul's time was almost up. People like Timothy gave Paul hope and confidence that the church would continue to grow under the leadership of those coming up behind him.

I also have a godly mother who spent her life loving and serving God. I do not doubt that the foundation she laid at the beginning of my life helped save my life on the day I flipped my motorcycle, and I am grateful.

Ahaziah did not have that legacy. His father had the distinction of being the most wicked king in Israel's history. His mother was the wicked witch of Israel who led Israel to worship idols. However, Ahaziah also knew who Elijah was, and Ahaziah could have been the one king who remembered the great works of God through Elijah and chose to take Israel in the right direction. He could have, but he did not.

"Now Ahaziah fell through the lattice of his upper room in Samaria, and was injured" (2 Kings 1:2a)

I first preached 2 Kings 1 over forty-six years ago at a church in Michigan, and I have loved this chapter ever since. This story generates controversy in the church because people are not really sure how to explain it.

Arthur Wallis reasoned, "When people do not like the literal meaning of something in the Bible, they are tempted to spiritualize it, and so rob it of its potency."

Was Ahaziah's fall nothing more than an unfortunate accident? Are there really any accidents? That is a great question, and it has been thoroughly explored by people more qualified than I am to explain their position. I will say that all of creation, including the laws of physics, serves the Lord and His purpose and is subject to His authority.

We may not know the exact reason or if there was a supernatural purpose behind Ahaziah's fall, but we know the result was injuries so severe that he was bedridden.

"What, Ahaziah?! Are you seriously going to ask a god named Baal after Jehovah has clearly demonstrated His sovereignty over all other gods?"

After forty-eight years in the ministry, one thing I know about people is that when the bottom falls out, when they are staring death in the face, they run to the god they really trust, whether it be a bottle, drugs, sex, or the Lord.

Ahaziah had a bad example, right? Who could really blame him for calling on the wrong god when he grew up in the middle of Baal worship? The problem with that thought is that Ahaziah knew who Elijah was. He knew him by sight. One of Ahaziah's men told him about a message from one of God's prophets, and as soon as he heard the physical description of this prophet, a hairy man wearing a leather belt, Ahaziah knew exactly who he was. He said, "That's Elijah the Tishbite."

Ahaziah knew about Jehovah and His prophet, but he simply chose to do his own thing, and his rebellion sent him on the road to his destruction, just like his parents. He did not humble himself. He did not reach out to Jehovah. He reached out to Baal-Zebub. This is the only Old Testament chapter in which Baal-Zebub is mentioned by name. We do not hear his name again until the New Testament, after Jesus drove demons out of a demon-possessed man.

Baal-Zebub was the fly god, the prince of demons, and this particular false god held a unique place of contempt among the Pharisees, so when they accused Jesus of working through the power of Baal-Zebub, that was a particularly scornful insult.

"But the angel of the LORD said to Elijah the Tishbite, 'Arise, go up to meet the messengers of the king of Samaria, and say to them, "Is it because there is no God in Israel that you are going to inquire of Baal-Zebub, the god of Ekron?" (2 Kings 1:3)

"I am the LORD, that is My name; and My glory I will not give to another, nor My praise to carved images." (Isaiah 42:8)

"Come on, Pastor Bill! No one prays to the fly god anymore."

Maybe not, but I know believers who read their horoscopes every day. They watch shows and movies rooted in the occult: witchcraft, astrology, psychics, tarot cards, etc. When we mess with that stuff, that is messing with the devil. He is our enemy. Why would we seek answers from him when all he wants to do is steal, kill, and destroy? Why would we ever seek answers to life's most difficult questions from a spiritually dead world?

I get so upset because God gets upset. He burns with jealousy for His people. I am not upset with the world. They do not know better until someone brings the Gospel into the dark world. I am upset with the children of the Light! We cannot and should not have any fellowship with the works of darkness. Is there not a God who saves, delivers, and heals His people?

Elijah intercepted Ahaziah's messengers, and he sent them back to Ahaziah with the Word of the Lord. The Lord was sending a warning.

"This says the Lord: Is it because there is no God in Israel that you are sending to inquire of Baal-Zebub, the god of Ekron? Therefore, you shall not come down from the bed to which you have gone up, but you shall surely die." (2 Kings 1:4)

Ahaziah's messengers delivered the message, word for word, but Ahaziah was unyielding, just like his parents.

I have sat down with many people at the end of their lives, and I am always amazed at how different their reactions are when they see the end approaching. Some hold fast to the Word. They examine and prepare their hearts. They serve God wholeheartedly until their last breath. Others leave this world in rebellion, their hearts full of bitterness and rage.

I cannot make the decision for anyone, but I can come with the message of truth. Only the Holy Spirit can change people's hearts; the catch is that they must allow Him to do so.

THE MAN WHO WOULD NOT RUN

"Then the king sent him a captain of fifty with his fifty men. So he went up to him, and there he was sitting on top of a hill. And he spoke to him: 'Man of God, the king has said, "Come down!" So Elijah answered him and said to the captain of fifty, 'If I am a man of God, then let the fire come down from heaven and consume you and your fifty men.' And fire came down from heaven and consumed him and his fifty." (2 Kings 1:9-10)

Elijah was not running anymore. Elijah found confidence and strength, not in his position as prophet of Israel, but in knowing his place in God. This kind of confidence did not come at the beginning of Elijah's story. It was the result of a lifetime of walking with God in the palace, by the brook, with the widow, on the mountain, in the cave... throughout his life. Elijah was not the same man who came off Mount Carmel. He was stronger. He knew God better, and he was not running anymore. God was on his side. His enemies did not have a chance!

I am not the same man who started Grace Church. I found my confidence in the Lord. I am secure in my position with

Him. God never lied to me, never abandoned me, and never destroyed me. His Word has never steered me wrong. He was faithful when I was faithless. I have watched Him stand by me week after week and year after year as I stand on His Word.

"None of these things move me; nor do I count my life as dear to myself, so that I may finish my race with joy, and the ministry which I received from the Lord Jesus, to testify to the gospel of the grace of God." (Acts 20:24)

"for I know whom I have believed and am persuaded that He is able to keep what I have committed to Him until that Day." (2 Timothy 1:12b)

God's Word says it far better than I ever could.

"Then he sent to him another captain of fifty with his fifty men. And he answered and said to him: 'Man of God, thus has the king said, "Come down quickly!"" So Elijah answered them and said to them, 'If I am a man of God, let fire come down from heaven and consume you and your fifty men. And the fire of God came down from heaven and consumed him and his fifty." (2 Kings 1:11-12)

The first group never returned. Their radios went silent. Maybe it was a bad idea to send a military squad against a man who called down fire from heaven, but sin makes people stupid, and Ahaziah tried again.

I do not know if Captain #2 had to step over charred bodies or if there were fifty-one burn spots on the ground where the first squad perished. I do not know if Captain #2 thought he could succeed where Captain #1 failed. Either way, he had to be one of the dumbest guys on the planet.

The church does not always know where to score this story on their theological charts. On the one hand, 1 Peter 2 says we must be law-abiding citizens, and these soldiers were simply carrying out their king's orders. On the other hand, if the law of the land violates or subverts the Word of God, the Word of God must reign in the lives of His followers, even if it brings about severe consequences.

The deaths of these men did not fall on the captains. The blame falls on the shoulders of Ahaziah. His defiance against God's Word and his worship of Baal-Zebub brought about the deaths of one hundred and two men who otherwise did not have to die.

The fallout of our sin directly impacts those around us, especially those closest to us, ensnaring them in the web of destruction we weave for ourselves.

"Again, he sent a third captain of fifty with his fifty men. And the third captain of fifty went up, and came and fell on his knees before Elijah, and pleaded with him, and said to him: 'Man of God, please let my life and the life of these fifty servants of yours be precious in your sight. Look, fire has now come down from heaven and burned up the first two captains of fifties with their fifties. But let my life now be precious in your sight." (2 Kings 1:13-14)

Captain #3 was given a fool's errand, but he did not act like a fool. He feared the Lord, and he respected the man of God. Captain #3 begged for mercy, and God granted his request. The fear of the Lord is the beginning of wisdom.

"And the angel of the LORD said to Elijah, 'Go down with him; do not be afraid of him. So he arose and went down with him to the king." (2 Kings 1:15)

Captain #3's humility and intercession spared not only his life but also the lives of the fifty men who were with him.

God sat with Elijah on the hill that day, just like He sat with him at the brook, on the mountain, in the cave, and now on the hill. Elijah would have to face another king who tried to kill him, but he knew he would be OK. Ahaziah was a defeated enemy.

"So Ahaziah died according to the word of the LORD which Elijah had spoken." (2 Kings 1:17)

Elijah outlasted all of his enemies. Two kings tried to destroy him. Two kings failed, but Elijah lived on, and the Word of God stood true and everlasting.

I could have never made it this far without the Word of God or the power of His Spirit in my life. The enemy of my soul tried to take me out, but he is a defeated enemy. Jesus took care of him on the cross, and now I walk in His victory. The Lord sent me out, hid me away, pruned me, and refined me. He led me to the peak of a mountain, where I could accomplish feats far beyond my strength. He lifted me up from a pit of despair. He renewed my heart, my spirit, my mind, and my life.

Nothing was done in my righteousness or strength. He accomplished everything according to His word and His promises for my life. I just said, "Yes. Here I am; send me."

I still have breath in my lungs. He has more in store, and He will finish what He started. I am not talking about becoming the greatest pastor or the most famous preacher on the radio or TV. I am talking about becoming the man God created me to be. I am talking about hearing those words, "Good and faithful servant."

I am a servant to His name, to His will, and to His Word. I am determined to finish, and God is determined to finish, and He promised to be with me to the very end, just like He was with Elijah.

Chapter Six

DEPARTURE

GOOD-BYE WORLD

GOING OUT

I once thought my last day was somewhere far beyond the horizon, but 65 years passed by in the blink of an eye. The sun is setting on my time here on earth, but whether I leave this place via the rapture or the grave, I will not die.

To be absent from the body is to be present with the Lord. Death is gain for a believer. Something special happens when I preach about the rapture. The hope of His appearing is the heartbeat of the church! We will see the Lord's face! The Holy Spirit reminds us, "Don't be ignorant." "Don't fall asleep."

Elijah's departure paints a vivid illustration of the rapture of the church. I always want to jump ahead to 2 Kings 2:11. Why slog through verses 1-10? Show me the chariot. Tell me about the whirlwind. Why not go to heaven the moment we receive salvation? Why go through all the other stuff?

Elijah knew the day of his departure, if not the hour, but he kept walking and working until the moment the chariot arrived. The Holy Spirit records Elijah's last conversation with his friend and student, Elisha, because relationships matter to God. People matter to God.

We go through all the other stuff because of people. We know where we are going, even if we do not know when. The Bible did say we would know the season, and as we see that season get closer, even as our own season on earth is coming to an end, it is all the more important to work with the same passion with which we entered the Kingdom as we had in the beginning, because God still wants to save people.

Scholars have speculated about the Lord's return for over 2000 years. None of their predictions came true. First, they said Jesus was coming back in 1976. Then we had "88 Reasons Why the Rapture Will Be in 1988" by Edgar C. Whisenant. Then we had Y2K. Lots of people believed them despite Matthew's writings that no one would know the day or hour, or Paul's writings that the day would come like a thief in the night.

Many of those people hunkered down and waited with end-of-the-world survival kits and underground shelters in place, but the date came and went. That is not how God wants His people to prepare or wait. Jesus encouraged His disciples, "Blessed is that servant whom his master, when he comes, will find so doing." (Matthew 24:46)

We wait by doing rather than watching and waiting. We do not stockpile supplies and hide. We go out. We tell people about Jesus. We minister to and sow into our relationships and the people the Lord has placed in our lives, and we work.

A LOYAL SERVANT AND FRIEND

"And it came to pass, when the LORD was about to take Elijah into heaven by a whirlwind, that Elijah went with Elisha from Gilgal. Then Elijah said to Elisha, 'Stay here, please, for the LORD has sent me on to Bethel." (2 Kings 2:1-2)

Elijah never faced another day alone after he left his cave of depression. Elisha was a true friend and loyal servant. Elijah tried to let Elisha off the hook. It is a strange exchange between master and servant, and I read at least nine commentaries trying to find out why Elijah would encourage Elisha to go his own way. We all agree that Elijah seemed to be testing Elisha.

Elisha would take over where Elijah left off, and Elijah had to know if Elisha was in because of the benefits their relationship provided him or if Elisha was committed to the word of the Lord and to see if Elisha truly loved Elijah. He wanted to know if Elisha would follow through until the end, even if it was hard and painful. Elisha was all in. He left everything behind and stayed in the fight because he loved his master and he loved his God.

There is no better feeling than knowing that someone is there because they want to be there, rather than for the benefits of the relationship.

Each Christmas, I send money to my daughter in another state, and she buys the toys that my grandchildren want before we get there. On Christmas day, they are so excited when they open their gifts, and my daughter reminds them, "Go thank Nanny and Papa. They give us a quick hug, and off they go to play. That is not wrong. They are just kids, and I will take all the hugs I can get. Sometimes, I will even bribe a hug, but that is not the same as those moments when my grandchildren snuggle up to me of their own accord simply because they want to be near us. That melts our hearts because we know that they are there because they love us.

Our Father needs to know how much we want to be with Him, not just because of what we get out of the deal, but because we love Him and have left everything behind to follow

Him. Sometimes, we need to sit at His feet and simply listen to what He wants to say instead of doing all the talking. It does something in our Father's heart when His children make a point of letting Him know how much we love Him.

GILGAL - ROLLING AWAY - SEPARATION FROM EGYPT AND THE WILDERNESS

"The LORD said to Joshua, 'This day I have rolled away the reproach of Egypt from you. Therefore, the name of the place is called Gilgal to this day." (Joshua 5:9)

Elijah spent his last day taking Elisha on a tour of significant landmarks in Israel's history. Elisha needed to know the foundation upon which his work would continue. Elijah had a great ministry, but the work of the Lord was there before Elijah, and it would continue after Elisha. God's Kingdom was bigger than both of them. It was even bigger than Israel.

This whole deal is bigger than the part we play. It is all about the Lord Jesus, and our finite minds cannot grasp the magnitude of what that means. It is important to know where we came from and how it all began. It is also important for us to share with our future generations the power of God's mighty hand and His Word because He is the same God who will move forward with them in their future works.

When Israel crossed the Jordan River, they arrived in Gilgal. Circumcision seemed like a strange way to commemorate the occasion, but Israel wanted to separate itself from the reproach of the wilderness. They wanted to leave Egypt behind. They wanted to separate themselves unto the Lord. Yes, separating ourselves means we have to remove something, but we remove it so that we make room for the Lord. As Israel circumcised their bodies, God hoped they would circumcise their hearts and set them apart for Him.

Circumcision did not save Israel any more than our works save us, but the physical act of obedience was an outward expression of their love and devotion to the Lord. Israel also celebrated Passover, remembering the moment when God delivered them from bondage.

Joshua circumcised Israel using knives he made out of flint. Praise God for Acts 15, which says we do not have to follow Israel in circumcision. The Holy Spirit circumcises our hearts using a knife that is sharper than any two-edged sword, the Word of God. It is so sharp that it cuts and separates the marrow from the joints. We follow the Lord in water baptism, not because the water saves us, but to outwardly express to the world the love that we have inside. These works tell the world that we want to be counted among those who follow Jesus.

Jesus separated us from the bondage and reproach of our past, and the Holy Spirit separates us unto God, making us a peculiar people and a holy nation.

We take communion to frequently remind ourselves of what the Lord did for us. We go back to the moment we crossed over from death in the wilderness into life everlasting in our Promised Land, which is the Lord Jesus. We cannot forget what the Lord has done for us because the moment we do; we can take His favor for granted. Gratitude often gives way to grumbling and complaining. An entire generation of Israelites perished in the wilderness because their love for God grew cold.

It is easy for faith and devotion to deteriorate into disbelief and contempt when we forget what the Lord has done for us. May we visit Gilgal often as we remember the moment when sin and shame were rolled away as we crossed over into a new life with the Lord Jesus.

BETHEL-THE HOUSE OF GOD

"Then Elijah said to Elisha, 'Stay here, please, for the LORD has sent me on to Bethel.' But Elisha said, "As the LORD lives, and as our soul lives, I will not leave you! So they went down to Bethel." (2 Kings 2:2)

The Lord communicated to Jacob in a dream, revealing a ladder that reached all the way up to heaven. God spoke to Jacob and gave him the same promise he gave to his grandfather, Abraham. The land on which he slept belonged to Jacob and his descendants. Not only that, but the hope of all mankind would come from his family. No wonder Jacob named that place, Bethel, which means, "The House of God." This was no ordinary place. God revealed Himself, and the stone upon which Jacob slept became a memorial.

Jacob eventually left that place, and when he did, his family became a mess. God told Jacob to go back to Bethel and make an altar. It was there that the Lord changed Jacob's name to Israel. God chose this place. God chose these people. Bethel played a significant role in the development of the patriarchs of our faith because it was a place of communion, consecration, and refuge. When they found themselves in need of a special encounter with God, they returned to Bethel, and God always welcomed them.

Sadly, Bethel, the House of God, became a house of idols. Elijah was about to leave it all behind, but Elisha would be left to represent the Lord to a nation that seemed determined to follow after the idols of their wicked kings. Sometimes, the courage to move forward comes from looking back and remembering what God has done for us and our people in the past. Bethel is where the roots of faith deepened in the lives of both Abraham and Jacob. Elisha would no longer have Elijah to turn to for help, but he could call on the name of the Lord whenever he needed it, just like his master and Israel's forefathers, and he would find God's help when he needed it.

I watch people discover Bethel in their hearts all the time. When new people start attending our Thursday night prayer meetings, I know right away that something is happening in their lives and that they want to hear from God. They want to build an altar of sacrifice and worship. It often takes a significant life event to bring them there.

No matter what brings us to the House of God, no matter how far we have run in the wrong direction or how big a mess we have made, we can always find our way to the altar of God and call His name. We will find forgiveness for our sins and help in our times of trouble.

JERICHO-THE PLACE OF WAR

"Then Elijah said to them, Elisha, stay here, please, for the LORD has sent me to Jericho. But he said, 'As the LORD lives, and as your soul lives, I will not leave you!" So they came to Jericho. Now the sons of the prophets who were at Jericho came to Elisha and said to him, "Do you know that the LORD will take away our master from you today?" So he answered, "Yes, I know; keep silent! (2 Kings 2:4-5)

Jericho was warfare. Joshua had to move forward without the advice or presence of his mentor and friend, Moses. The future of Israel rested on the shoulders of Joshua. The responsibility of leading God's people into their promised land was now his burden to carry. The people of Jericho were stronger and bigger, and they were protected by a wall that seemed impenetrable. However, there was none stronger or greater than God, and there was no wall strong enough or tall enough to withstand the will of God and the power of His Word.

Israel's promise did not die with Moses. It lived on in God's Word, and Joshua served the same God that Moses did. Joshua's mentor passed away. Elisha's mentor would be carried away. Unless the rapture happens in my lifetime, I will pass away. The Good News is that God's Word will endure forever.

Jericho taught Israel how to fight. Victory did not depend on the man. It depended on God and His Word. God told Israel to march in silence around Jericho every day for six days, and on the seventh day, they were to march seven times. They were to remain silent until the Lord told them to "shout, for the Lord has given them the city." If God promised, then it was done. Elisha may face battles, too, but the Lord fights for His people.

God still fights for His people, and our weapons are the same: The Word of God and the Name of God. Our enemy does not fight fair, but we have a Champion in the Lord Jesus who has already defeated the enemy. Jesus showed us how to win our battles by submitting to the Word of God. It is not by might or by power, but by the Spirit of God. Our weapons are mighty through God for the pulling down of strongholds. God uses us to destroy the works of the enemy by the authority of His Word, the power of His Name, and the presence of His Spirit. We put on the whole armor of God, and we withstand the attacks of our enemy. We fight back with the Sword of the Spirit. Elijah, Moses, Abraham, Joshua, and Jacob were all just human beings with a nature like our own, but they served a Mighty God. We serve a Mighty God.

THE NEXT GENERATION

"Now the sons of the prophets who were at Jericho came to Elisha and said to him, 'Do you know that the LORD will take away your master from over you today?" (2 Kings 2:5)

There was a group of young prophets who joined up with Elijah and Elisha at some point. These young prophets were eager to use their gifts, but they got ahead of themselves. They had not yet developed discernment on when to speak and blurt out everything they know or when to simply be a comforting presence on someone's hardest day. Elisha knew the truth, but that did not make it any less painful to be separated from someone he cared about so deeply.

We have all been there on those days when we know the Lord is good, but we also know what we dread the most will soon happen. We do trust God, but that does not mean the pain is not real. I pray for discernment in those moments when I know I am about to walk in on someone in the middle of their worst day, so that instead of trying to be a great prophet of God, I will have the discernment to simply be a comforting presence as I sit with them when that moment arrives.

JORDAN-THE PLACE OF GOODBYE

"Then Elijah said to him, 'Stay here, please, for the LORD has sent me on to the Jordan. But he said, 'As the Lord lives, and as your soul lives, I will not leave you! So the two of them went on. And fifty men of the sons of the prophets went and stood facing them at a distance, while the two of them stood by the

Jordan. Now Elijah took his mantle, rolled it up, and struck the water; and it was divided this way and that, so that the two of them crossed over on dry ground." (2 Kings 2:6-8)

The Jordan was the last obstacle that stood between Israel and their Promised Land, and when the Israelites arrived there, water overran the riverbanks. It looked like the end of the road for Israel. The Jordan often alludes to death in the Scriptures, and it derives from the Hebrew word yarden, which translates as "the descent." The Jordan, however, was not the end for Israel.

The priests stepped into the river with the Ark of the Covenant, and the river opened up, creating a path on which Israel crossed over and finally set foot on the promise that carried them out of Egypt and into the new life that awaited them.

I have officiated all kinds of funerals, including far too many for young people. Our days on earth are numbered, but for those who follow Jesus, death is not the end. When Jesus Christ stepped in, death opened up, and those who pass from this life simply walk across into the long-awaited Promised Land of heaven. It will be the end of our old life, but it will also be the beginning of our new, eternal life.

The sun was setting on Elijah's time on earth, and he would soon part ways with his dear friend, but this was not the end for Elijah. Elijah struck the same river with his mantle, and the waters parted, just like they did for Israel all those years ago. This whole journey was set up to remind Elisha of the God they served.

Israel had an awesome past with the Lord. Elijah had an awesome past with the Lord, but God's glory days were not over. They would continue in the men and women who would be willing to answer the call, take up the mantle, and follow the Lord.

Elisha could have stayed on the side of the Jordan where all the other prophets stood and watched from afar, but Elisha was determined to follow his master to the very end. Elisha was moving onto a greater anointing, but the crowd could not go.

They do not always mean to, but the crowd, even the crowd in the church, will discourage us from stepping into the unique call that God has placed on our lives. Many people were content with watching Jesus from afar, but Jesus said, "If anyone desires to come after Me, let him deny himself, take up his cross, and follow Me." (Matthew 16:24)

This may have been the end of Elijah and Elisha's time together, but this was also the beginning of what God would do in and through Elisha.

"And so it was, when they had crossed over, that Elijah said to Elisha, 'Ask! What may I do for you, before I am taken away from you?' Elisha said, 'Please let a double portion of your spirit be upon me." (2 Kings 2:9)

Elisha felt the weight of the responsibility that accompanied the call of God. Elisha knew he needed the Lord's help. He knew his inadequacy, and he did not rely on his own strength, wisdom, abilities, or experience to carry on with the work of God. He not only wanted what Elijah had, but he wanted more; he wanted double. He needed the Spirit of God.

It was not Elijah's strength or wisdom that made Elijah a great prophet of God; it was the Spirit of God that rested upon and flowed through the man of God.

"So he said, "You have asked a hard thing. Nevertheless, if you see me when I am taken from you, it shall be so for you; but if not, it shall not be so. Then it happened, as they continued on and talked, that suddenly a chariot of fire appeared with horses of fire, and separated the two of them; and Elijah went up by a whirlwind into heaven." (2 Kings 2:10-11)

Of course, Elijah wanted to grant his request because he loved Elisha, but the favor and the anointing of God were not his to give. God gives spiritual gifts as He sees fit. It would have been one thing to be chosen by Elijah, but when Elisha saw the chariot, he knew that God Himself had chosen him, and God would give him exactly what he asked for. Knowing this raised Elisha's confidence to a whole new level. It is one thing to be chosen by our mentors, but it is another to be chosen by God.

Though it did not feel like it at the time, Elijah's departure was a good thing for Elisha. The Bible recorded seven miracles from Elijah's ministry, but it recorded fourteen from Elisha's ministry. God honored Elisha's desire for a double anointing. Elijah had passed on his legacy of praying bold prayers!

Jesus said that it would be good for Him to go away so he could send the Holy Spirit. Jesus told His disciples they would do even greater works than He did because the Holy Spirit would send them to all parts of the world. Jesus was Emmanuel, God with us. The Holy Spirit would be God in us.

HIS WAYS ARE NOT OURS

Praise God that He did not answer Elijah's request to let him die under the broom tree. God said "No" because He already knew the end from the beginning. By the time the whirlwind arrived, all of life's sorrows and disappointments had disappeared in the flames of that chariot.

Over the years, I have become just as thankful for the "no" answers as I am for the "yes" answers because God knew so much more than I did. The three greatest days in a believer's life are the day they are born, the day of salvation, and the day they die.

We all know how it starts, with birth. We all know how it ends. We all die. What we do not know is how it all plays out in the middle. Unexpected things will happen, and Jesus told us life would be hard, not easy.

For Elijah, it ended in a whirlwind. It will end for us with a wedding to the Son of God, who has spent the middle preparing a place for us. He is as eager for us to arrive as we are to go! We all endure the same kind of witches, the same kind of broom tree, and the same kind of trials, but we also know that if we follow to the end, we will end up in heaven when it is all over.

Elijah lived his last day as obediently and abundantly as he did on the first day we met him in the courts of Ahab. He wanted to cross the finish line with nothing left to give because he spent all of his energy and resources on building a Kingdom that would last forever. The man who prayed under the broom tree was not kicking back in a cave anymore, and I do not want to spend my last days kicking back in a recliner. When the sun sets on our last days on earth, it will rise on our first day in glory, and I want to know that I finished my race with nothing left to give because I gave it all, just like my Savior gave it all for me.

ONE LAST MIRACLE

"Now Elijah took his mantle, rolled it up, and struck the water, and it was divided this way and that, so the two of them crossed over on dry land." (2 Kings 2:8)

Elijah was eager to demonstrate God's power and authority to Elisha and the young prophets who were watching him. He did not hit the water just to hit the water. This was some Moses and Joshua action! Israel had come a long way from its days of captivity in Egypt and its battle against Jericho, but Israel was moving in the wrong direction. Many prophets had been killed, and most of the kings abandoned God's Word.

This young generation needed a fresh understanding of the God of Israel. The Red Sea did not part because of Moses. Joshua did not roll back the Jordan River. Elijah did not rain down fire on Mount Carmel. Understand me when I say these were great men of God, but their greatness derived solely from their willingness to follow God and obey His command.

God was the one who parted the sea. God was the one who rolled back the Jordan. God was the one who rained down fire.

"Then he took the mantle of Elijah that had fallen from him, and struck the water and said, "Where is the LORD God of Elijah?" And when he also had struck the water, it was divided this way and that; and Elisha crossed over." (2 Kings 2:14)

Elijah's last miracle was Elisha's first miracle. The same God who empowered Moses, Joshua, and Elijah now empowers Elisha. Jehovah was the God of Israel's past, present, and future. Elijah's time ended, but God's work was not finished.

He is the same miracle-working God. The God of Abraham, Jacob, Moses, Joshua, Elijah, and Elisha is also the God of Bill Gehm and of Grace Church. We fight a good fight from a place of victory, not to our glory but to the glory of Jesus Christ, who has already overcome! The Lord ascended into heaven, but He left us with the Holy Spirit who rests upon us, empowering us to work until the end.

A SERVANT UNTIL THE END

"Elijah said unto Elisha, "Ask! What may I do for you before I am taken from you?" (2Kings 2:9)

Let us run until we cross the finish line. The end is not a place to get comfortable and take it easy. We do not slow down. As long as we have breath, we serve the Kingdom.

Hey, old guys! Ask the younger generation how we can serve them.

Hey, young guys! Listen to the old guys as they pass on their wisdom and experience.

I want to hand off what I know about the Lord. I want to take other people to the places I have been with God. I want to show them what I have seen in God.

I do not know what will happen to Grace Church and Radio by Grace when I am gone.

It has been my life and my heart, but it has never been about my name or my glory. It is about the Lord. It is about His name and His legacy. I do know it will be hard to separate from the work I love and the people I love. But I do know the church is in good hands because I know the hearts of the men and women coming up behind me. I know they call on the Lord. I know they depend on the Lord. They are loyal to His Name and His Word. I know the same God who did exceedingly above what I ever imagined will do the same for them.

God wants me to invest in and serve the future generations that are coming up behind me. The greatest leader in history served His people and laid down His life for them. I want to follow His example.

TAKE UP THE MANTLE

"Then it happened, as they continued on and talked, that suddenly a chariot of fire appeared with the horses of fire, and separated the two of them, and Elijah went up by the whirlwind into heaven." (2 Kings 2:11)

Minutes became seconds as Elijah and Elisha walked together in fellowship, but Elijah's time was up. Elisha watched his master climb higher and higher until he was out of sight, crying, My father, my father! Elijah was his spiritual father, and his heart was broken so badly at Elijah's departure that he tore his own clothes in two. Elisha's request for a double portion, which was the privilege of the firstborn son in Jewish tradition, was granted by God. Though Elijah left Elisha, Elisha was not alone, for the Lord was with him, just as he had been with his mentor.

God did not leave Elisha without comfort or hope. He left Elisha with Elijah's mantle and the Holy Spirit's anointing. He left him with the school of prophets so he would not have to carry out his ministry or live out the rest of his time on earth alone.

"He took up the mantle of Elijah that had fallen from him, and went back and stood by the bank of the Jordan. Then he took the mantle of Elijah that had fallen from him, and struck the water, and said, 'Where is the LORD God of Elijah?' And when he had also struck the water, it was divided this way and that; and Elisha crossed over." (2 Kings 2:13-15)

Nothing happened until Elisha picked up the mantle. Elisha would have to step out in faith before he could step into his anointing. He had never struck the river before. What if it did not work for him? Elisha may have felt foolish, but when Elisha stepped out in obedience and faith, the Holy Spirit stepped in with His strength and His power.

Jesus spent His last moments before the crucifixion with His disciples, the boys who had walked with Him for the past three years. He had so much to pass on, but time moved quickly, and suddenly, Jesus was walking down the road of suffering to the cross. That was His road and His alone.

After His resurrection, Jesus' followers watched Him ascend into heaven, and continued looking until he was out of sight. What would they do now?

Jesus gave them instructions to meet together and wait in Jerusalem until the Holy Spirit fell upon them. That is still Christ's gift to His church. We can appreciate the Holy Spirit. We can even agree with the Holy Spirit. We can stand by and watch Him fall on the people around us, but nothing will happen for us until we reach out and take hold of the promised Holy Spirit for ourselves.

God did not leave us alone. He left us the Holy Spirit. He left us the church.

We will be caught up into the air to meet Jesus in the same manner as Elijah.

"And thus shall we always be with the Lord. Therefore, comfort one another with these words." (1 Thessalonians 4:17b-18)

That day is coming!

What should we do in the meantime, Pastor Bill?

Remember that day. Speak of it often. Encourage each other. Comfort each other. Walk together as we follow the Lord. Step up and receive the Holy Spirit. Get to work. Represent the Lord. Remember the words of Jesus.

"Blessed is that servant whom his master, when he comes, will find so doing."

(Matthew 24:46)

Chapter Seven

DYNAMICS

THE LEGACY OF FAITH

MAKE IT COUNT

Everyone wants their lives to count. We search everywhere to find meaning and purpose for our existence. The truth is, we were created for a purpose, but to discover that purpose, we must entrust our lives into the hands of the One who created us. We live, move, and have our being because of Him. The good news is that no life is insignificant. God notices every sparrow that falls from the sky, and we are worth so much more than a sparrow.

Our time on earth does have a shelf life, but we are living stones that are being built into an eternal Kingdom. We serve an immortal King, and our works serve His purpose, which is everlasting. No life lived in service to Jesus Christ is wasted. No child of God is a "miscellaneous person." No work completed or sacrifice offered to the Lord is meaningless. God keeps track of it all.

One summer night during my sabbatical, I decided to drive straight through to our next destination. Cindy slept, and I listened to the radio. As I drove out of St. Louis, I came across a preacher at 2 am, and I recognized the voice of J. Vernon

McGee, one of the original radio preachers. I like him, and I have listened to him often through the years.

This particular broadcast was from when he was a younger man in his thirties. Seventy years or so later, in the dead of night, on a deserted road in the middle of nowhere, God used J. Vernon McGee to minister to me and help give direction to my life. I was guided and blessed by a man who lived faithfully to God, and the impact of his ministry lived on even though he had passed over forty years ago.

A few years ago, I received a letter from a fourteen-year-old girl in Kentucky who heard my broom tree sermons on the radio and said God used them in her life as she sat under her own broom tree. I wrote a children's book called Monster Billy, and this girl wrote a sequel inspired by my struggle with depression. My wife and I stopped in Kentucky on one of our vacations and connected with her and her mother. They blessed me, and we blessed them simply because God's Word and His Kingdom are vast and extend far beyond our time on earth or the boundaries of our communities.

People live-stream our services from all over. God projects His voice through Grace Church and Radio By Grace all across the world, not because of me or my staff, but because it is His Word. God does whatever He wills with the seeds we sow. His Spirit hovers over all of it, watering and tending to it, and He produces all kinds of fruit from all kinds of fields. If we could understand and if I could effectively communicate how God can take our commitment to His Kingdom and His Word, even the smallest acts of obedience, and use them to impact eternity, we would never serve God halfheartedly.

JESUS WENT TO CHURCH

"So He came to Nazareth, where He had been brought up. And as His custom was, He went into the synagogue on the Sabbath day, and stood up to read." (Luke 4:16)

It is hard to imagine that Jesus could benefit at all from the church when He literally wrote the book, but the church was about more than the sermons. God never intended for man to carry out the work of God alone. Community and fellowship were part of God's design, and they were important to Jesus. Much had transpired in the life of Jesus, and He was eager to get home and share with the people He knew and loved at His home church.

God created the first covenant community way back in the Garden of Eden when He created the covenant of marriage. Adam and Eve tended the Garden together. Corporate worship was a big part of Israel's Old Covenant. Not even the Son of God would attempt to carry out the work of God alone. He created a community with His disciples.

The writer of Hebrews drives home this point when he admonishes believers to gather as often as they can. Hebrews is all about the better covenant, which is the Lord Jesus.

Community is part of the Kingdom, and the church is a good thing. We come together and worship. We gather around God's Word. We carry out the work of God together. We take what we learn in church out into the world, which needs our message. We invite them to become part of this new and better Covenant with the Lord. The Kingdom has never been about one person. It is about the Lord Jesus, and Jesus demonstrated the importance of gathering with the Lord's people.

JESUS OPENS THE BOOK

"And He was handed the book of the prophet Isaiah. And when He had opened the book, He found the place where it was written:" (Luke 4:17)

Jesus opened the Book. He stuck to the Book.

When we gather together, we'd better open the Book. We do not come to hear the thoughts and opinions of a man. We do not pick and choose which parts of the Book are important. It is all important, not just the verses we like. We go through the entire Book, from Genesis to Revelation and everything in between, and we are careful not to miss a single word from the Word of God. The Book is our foundation, instruction, and inspiration, and we receive our revelations from the words in the Book.

"The Spirit of the Lord GOD is upon Me, because the LORD has anointed Me to preach the good tidings to the poor; He has sent Me to heal the brokenhearted, to proclaim liberty to the captives, and the opening of the prison to those who are bound; to proclaim the acceptable year of the LORD," (Isaiah 61:1-2a)

Prior to this sermon, in Luke 3, John the Baptist baptized Jesus, and when he did, the Holy Spirit came down in the form of a dove and landed on Jesus. The original text used the Greek word *epi*, which means upon. The Holy Spirit came upon Jesus before He delivered the message. If Jesus needed the Holy Spirit to preach the Word of God, how much more do we need Him? I believe in the Ghost. I need the Ghost to come upon me, and I pray for Him to descend and come upon me before I deliver my sermons.

THE DIVINE REVELATION

"Then he closed the book, gave it back to the attendant, and sat down. And the eyes of all who were in the synagogue were fixed on Him. And He began to say to them, today this Scripture is fulfilled in your hearing." (Luke 4:20-21)

Jesus stopped in the middle of verse 2. Why? Because Jesus knew exactly what He was doing. The day of vengeance was not part of His first advent. This was a day of hope! For years, Israel had waited for their Messiah, and now He stood in the midst of them. How blessed they were to hear Him speak that day. If only they would open their hearts to Him, their eyes would see the salvation of their God. Their ears would hear the Word of the Lord.

How blessed we are here in America! We live where the Word of God is freely accessible, and many have heard the Gospel dozens, maybe even hundreds, of times. I pray our hearts are open every time we hear the Word of God preached. It is a sacred privilege we have. Hear Him. Do not miss Him. Do not ignore Him. He is the Way, the Truth, and the Life, and He is standing in front of us. We have heard the Word of the Lord, and today, here and now, is the day of salvation.

THE MARVEL

"So all bore witness to Him, and marveled at the gracious words which proceeded out of His mouth." (Luke 4:22a)

Everyone had to decide that day. Was he really Israel's hope? Was he the anointed one they had been waiting for? Luke 4:22 asks, "Is this not Joseph's son?"

Is He really our Savior? Is He the Lord? Are His Words really truth and life?

From the day He arrived, people have always marveled at Jesus, even in our culture today. His teachings are as counterculture as they get. Most people respect Him. Some even appreciate the lessons He taught, but that is about it. His words have wisdom, but they are not the truth.

They believe Him to be a great man with great ideas, a great teacher. Some believe that maybe even a great prophet. But respect is not the same thing as reverence. Marvel is not the same thing as surrender. At some point, we all must decide what we are going to do with the truth once we have heard it.

"He said to them, You will surely say this proverb to Me, 'Physician, heal yourself! Whatever we have heard done in Capernaum, do also here in Your country." (Luke 4:23)

God's Word never made its way into Israel's heart. They remained hardhearted and stiff-necked. Israel expected a Messiah who would validate their own superiority to the rest of the world because they were convinced of their own righteousness. Jesus challenged their understanding of what true righteousness was.

They tried to impress each other with their eloquent prayers, but God was not impressed. While they paraded their righteous deeds in front of each other, they secretly plotted how to cheat and oppress. Jesus called them out. He exposed the true condition of their hearts, and they hated Him for it.

The righteous elite had contempt for the poor and the weak. Jesus moved away from the priests and the Pharisees. By contrast, He moved towards the sinners, outcasts, and the "unclean". They despised Him for healing a blind beggar. They detested Him for eating with tax collectors. They scorned Him for rescuing an adulterous woman.

They could not accept that there was no one righteous, not a single one, not even the descendants of Abraham. Jesus did not come to exclude anyone. He opened up God's Kingdom to anyone who would receive it: priests, tax collectors, lepers, blind men, widows, sinners-anyone who wanted to be saved.

He came to destroy the works of darkness and shine His holy light. He came to save, deliver, and heal. He came to set captives free, to bring hope to the poor, and Israel had first dibs on all of it. Jesus fulfilled the law of Moses. He came to save Israel, but they closed their eyes, covered their ears, and hardened their hearts.

JESUS, A PROPHET, AND A WIDOW

"But I tell you truly, many widows were in Israel in the days of Elijah, when the heaven was shut up three years and six months, and there was a great famine throughout all the land; but to none of them was Elijah sent except to Zarephath, in the region of Sidon, to a woman who was a widow," (Luke 4:25-26)

Elijah's life was filled with so many amazing stories that it makes sense that Jesus would use him at some point to drive home His message. One thing all of Israel could agree on was that Elijah was a great prophet. There was the story about the time Elijah busted into Ahab's court. There was the story about the ravens and the brook. What about when fire fell from heaven? That was the greatest story, right? But Jesus did not use any of those stories. He chose the story of a Gentile widow.

This seemed like the most insignificant era in Elijah's timeline, but it was not insignificant to Jesus. Yes, Elijah mattered, but so did this Gentile widow. Her story was not inconsequential. She may have been but a small chapter in 1 Kings, but her faith and obedience to the Lord made an impression, and He used her story to drive home His point.

Elijah came to her with a message of hope, much like Jesus did on the day He preached in the synagogue. However, instead of trusting her own wisdom and understanding, she trusted in the prophet's message because it offered hope and life in a dead and hopeless climate.

She listened to the message, and she surrendered everything, even when it went against "common sense." Consequently, she witnessed resurrection power in both her life, the prophet's life, and her son's life. She was an illustration of things to come.

The Gentiles embraced Jesus. They embraced the cross. They took God's Word into their hearts, and they received the Good News of Jesus. Just like the widow realized that the God of Elijah was her only hope, so did the Gentiles realize that Israel's rejection of Jesus was their shot at receiving salvation and being grafted in as children of God. They witnessed God's resurrection power.

One day, God will remove the scales from Israel's eyes. God will finish what He started and fulfill His promise to Abraham. Israel will receive her Messiah. I constantly pray for Israel. I pray for Gentiles too. Anyone can be saved.

Elijah had no idea that the Son of God would use his life in a sermon to His home church 750 years later. The widow from Zarephath could not have known that He would use her as an illustration of the hope that would soon come to the Gentiles.

They were people who simply followed and obeyed the Lord and His Word to the best of their ability.

May we continue to work for the Lord with all of our hearts, with a new understanding that the Lord's Word always accomplishes its purpose and that a life wasted at the feet of Jesus is no life wasted at all. He deserves it. He receives it. He uses it. And he is most definitely worth it.

THE WORK OF PRAYER

"Elijah was a man with a nature like ours, and he prayed earnestly that it would not rain; and it did not rain on the land for three years and six months. And he prayed again, and the heaven gave rain, and the earth produced its fruit." (James 5:17-18)

James ' devotion to prayer earned him the nickname "Camel Knees" by early church historian Hegesippus because of the callouses his knees developed from hours spent in prayer. James, one of the greatest prayer warriors in the New Testament church, tagged Elijah as one of the greatest prayer warriors in the Old Testament.

I know we touched briefly on prayer in the beginning, but I feel it is such a vital force in the church of Jesus Christ that we need to spend more time examining the work of prayer.

People ask me all the time, "How do I know what I am supposed to do for God?

I cannot tell anyone their spiritual gift, but I can dogmatically say that every follower of Jesus Christ is called to the work of prayer. Jesus Christ dedicated Himself to prayer. His followers must be dedicated to prayer as well.

Years ago, Stanley Construction hired me as a laborer. They handed me a yellow work hat and a shovel and told me, "It's time to go to work!" Some of the guys on my crew held the same standard-issue shovel in their hands and wore the same standard-issue hat on their heads, but when it came time to work, they leaned on the shovel. They may have dug in occasionally, removing a small amount of dirt here and there, but others dug their shovel in from the time they punched in until the time to leave, doing exactly what the boss asked them to do. We are saved by faith and saved to do good works. Both are true, and we go about the Father's business until Jesus returns.

Prayer is one of the most neglected jobs we do and one of the most underused tools we have to accomplish what God wants to accomplish through His church. It is time for the church to punch in, get on our knees, and go to work, laboring in prayer for the world around us.

THE FATHER'S BUSINESS

"Is anyone among you sick? Let him call for the elders of the church, and let them pray over him, anointing him with oil in the name of the Lord. And the prayer of faith will save the sick, and the Lord will raise him up. And if he has committed sins, he will be forgiven. Confess your trespasses to one another, and pray for one another, that you may be healed. The effective, fervent prayer of a righteous man avails much." (James 5:14-16)

Our business is people because God's business is people. Jesus died to save people. Jesus interceded and still intercedes for people. People are the reason we pray, not just for the climate, but for the people who live in the climate. We pray not just because of war but also because of the people who are impacted by it. We dig in our shovels, and we go to work, praying for the people in our lives, praying for the people who are in need, and praying that the world would wake up and see that they need a Savior.

We do not often pray like Elijah, James, or Jesus. We talk too much about the casual, "hanging out with God" type of relationship. Hear me when I say that I love hanging out with God. He is my friend. But there is an unseen realm, and there is a war going on for the souls of mankind. We need the effective and fervent prayers of God's men and women. The words effective and fervent come from the Greek word *energeo*, which means "to work", "to put forth effort", or "to aid".

Elijah prayed for God to shut up the heavens so that Israel would remember God. He prayed for the widow's son so that she would keep her faith in God. He prayed for the fire to fall so that Israel would turn back to God. Elijah prayed for rain so that there would be revival in Israel. Elijah's prayers were about more than just his needs and desires.

We need men and women who will pray with all their hearts and storm the gates of heaven. We need believers who will tap into the power of God, who has the power to change everything.

"Elijah was a man with a nature like ours, and he prayed earnestly that it would not rain; and it did not rain on the land for three years and six months. And he prayed again, and the heaven gave rain, and the earth produced its fruit." (James 5:17-18)

The text uses two Greek words, *proseuchomai* and *proseuche*. He prayed, and then he prayed again. It is the root from which we derive the words "advocate" and "lawyer". I say it like this: "With a prayer, he did pray." He prayed for help so that he could pray.

Elijah did not offer up a token prayer, but he brought his case to God.

Jesus told a story in Luke 18 about a widow who wanted justice from an unjust judge who refused to help her. The widow was relentless in pleading her case, and the judge caved simply because she refused to back down. She had a need, and the judge was the only one who could help.

We have an advocate before the Father. He even paid our penalty for sin so that we could go before the Father to plead our case. Fervent and persistent prayers avail much because our God is all about a relationship with His people, and Jesus restored our freedom to go straight to the Father, where we can find grace, mercy, and help in times of need. The Thessalonians say we can pray about everything.

So, we pray, and not just token prayers that check off a religious box. Our judge is not only fair, but He also loves us. God the Son stands beside us and advocates for us. God, the Holy Spirit steps in and prays for us when we do not know how to pray or what to pray for. The fullness of the Trinity is present and active, all working together in unity for our good because God loves us. Psalm 116 says God inclines His ear to us when we pray. God Almighty moves towards the sound of our voices when His people call upon Him. Why would we not pray, and pray, and pray?

TAKING OUR MEDICINE

"Is anyone among you suffering? Let him pray. Is anyone cheerful? Then let him sing psalms. Is anyone among you sick? Let him call for the elders of the church, and let them pray over him, anointing him with oil in the name of the Lord. And the prayer of faith will save the sick, and the Lord will raise him up. And if he has committed sins, he will be forgiven." (James 5:13-15)

Prayer warriors, those who do the work of prayer, make prayer their first response to everything. They cry out to God before they call the preacher. They start singing in their hearts before they go to church. God wants to talk to us, and He wants us to talk to Him. God wants to be first in our hearts, minds, and lives, and He wants to be the first one we go to about anything. I would not label myself a prayer warrior, but I am growing in the work of prayer.

We pray first, separately, in our closets, but God's people also come together and pray. Sometimes we get weak or tired. We lose our strength. The Greek word for sick is *astheneo*, which translates as weak, feeble, or powerless. When that happens, James instructs us to call for the elders of the church and let them pray. I still believe in elders. I believe in anointing people with oil because the oil represents the Holy Spirit. It is part of our medicine.

We confess our sins to each other and pray for each other. We don't have to confess only to the pastor. Everyone should belong to a group, a fellowship of believers. We need accountability. We need help. Life is still hard, even when we are saved. We struggle with sin, even though we're saved. We are not in heaven yet, but we can connect with those who belong to the Kingdom of God here on earth and carry each other's burdens in prayer.

HOUSE OF PRAYER

"Then Jesus went into the temple of God and drove out all those who bought and sold in the temple, and overturned the tables of the money changers and the seats of those who sold doves. And He said to them, It is written, 'My house shall be called a house of prayer," but you have made it a "den of thieves. (Matthew 21:12-13)

Jesus felt strongly about the integrity of the Temple, and passion for God's House consumed Him. According to the Leviticus Law, a holy law given by God, the people were required to bring a sacrifice to the Temple. Because many people traveled to Jerusalem from other places, they waited until they arrived in Jerusalem to purchase their sacrifice.

The money changers exploited this law and drove up the prices on the Temple sacrifices, especially on doves or pigeons, by as much as twenty times the original cost, kind of like when we spend $6 for a Coke at the movies. They exploited the poor and gouged those who faithfully honored God's law. God's House became a place for profit rather than for what God originally intended.

The Tabernacle and the Temple were both designed as places for God to meet with His people and reveal Himself and His glory. Their priorities were all messed up, and Jesus went in to clean house. He tossed out what needed to go. He looked and sounded a lot like Elijah.

Jesus did not want to destroy the people. He desired to rebuild the Temple, which represented His Father, a place where people drew near to God and He drew near to them. God's house was to be a house of prayer.

As glorious as the Temple and the Tabernacle were, they were temporary. Hebrews revealed that they were shadows, but Jesus Christ became the substance. Jesus Christ embodied the entirety of God's glory. Jesus, Emmanuel, met with His people.

When God saved us, we became the Temple of the Holy Spirit, and sometimes our priorities get out of whack. We forget the purpose for which we were created. He may need to kick over some tables and chairs in our hearts and drive out what does not belong. I pray, "Lord Jesus, overturn and kick up anything You need to in order to restore my heart to what it should be." I represent the Lord. We represent the Lord, and God's people pray. We are a house of prayer.

ASK

"Now in the morning, as He returned to the city, He was hungry. And seeing a fig tree by the road. He came to it and found nothing on it but leaves, and said to it, 'Let no fruit grow on you ever again. Immediately, the fig tree withered away. And when the disciples saw it, they marveled, saying, "How did the fig tree wither away so soon?" So Jesus answered and said to them, 'Assuredly, I say to you, if you have faith and do not doubt, you will not only do what was done to the fig tree, but also if you say to this mountain, "Be removed and be cast into the sea," it will be done. And whatever things you ask in prayer, believing, you will receive." (Matthew 21:18-22)

The fig tree was guilty of false advertising. The leaves promised delicious fruit, but when Jesus got there, there was nothing. No fruit. Jesus performed only two destructive miracles, none involving people: He cast demons into the swine and cursed the fig tree that yielded no fruit. As the disciples marveled at the tree's demise, Jesus let them in on a Kingdom secret. Our prayers, coupled with our faith, can accomplish mighty things, things that we think are impossible, even something as impossible as moving a mountain. Jesus already told them this in Matthew 17:21.

Our prayers, plus even a tiny bit of faith, as tiny as a mustard seed, can yield powerful results. How? Our tiny bit of faith is planted and rooted in Almighty God. My prayers plus my tiny seed of faith can move a mountain. That is how.

Years ago, we faced a mountain-sized problem in our church. We outgrew our old building on Amarillo Boulevard, and we needed to add on to make more room in our church. Our building sat on top of a hill, and behind our building, it dropped off dramatically, so we made inquiries into bringing in dirt. We needed a bunch of dirt, and I was never one for taking up building fund collections. I did not want to ask for a "drywall offering", much less a "mountain of dirt" offering. The amount of money we needed to raise seemed as high as the mountain of dirt we needed to bring in.

The surveyor looked around and said, "You need a ton of dirt everywhere!" and I was immediately discouraged..

I was due to preach at the retirement home, but before I left, God reminded me of the sermon I just preached that previous Sunday from Matthew 17:20: "If you have faith as a mustard seed, you will say to this mountain, "Move from here to there,' and it will move; and nothing will be impossible for you." I prayed that morning with my tiny seed of faith prayer, "Lord, we literally need that mountain moved," and I went on my way.

When I came back to my office later that day, I found a business card along with this note on my desk.

Bill, call this man when you get this note. He has some dirt he wants to bring over. He's been here twice.

I had only been gone for just over an hour. Of course, I called right away, and he was already in the parking lot for the third time.

I asked him, "What's wrong with this dirt? Is it radioactive?"

He answered me, "Nothing."

Then I asked the question I always hate the most, "How much?"

He replied, "Nothing."

Honestly, I did not think much of it after that. I was grateful, and in my mind, it was a great start. I thanked God, "Some free dirt is better than nothing." Little faith..

I prayed for dirt.

All day on Thursday, there were bulldozers clearing out the fields behind our church. The cost to us was...zero, nothing. I drove into work Friday morning, and there was a traffic jam all the way from the middle of Bell Street leading up to Amarillo Boulevard, where semi trucks after semi trucks filled with dirt lined up to turn into the parking lot of Grace Church.

I called my guys, "You've gotta get down here! You have to see this!"

This went on and on until the mountain was completed. Tiny faith. Big God. Our tiny faith in our big God moved that mountain. The answers to our prayers do not ride on us, our abilities, or our power. They are seeds of faith planted in a God who can do more than we even know to ask for.

Whenever I feel discouraged or like it is hopeless, when I come up against a mountain that I need God to move, I drive to that old property, and I remember what God did for me then. I still pray to the same God, and He still moves mountains on my behalf.

Elijah prayed for God to shut up the heavens. He prayed for rain. He prayed for a dead boy. Elijah got what he prayed for.

I got the dirt, but getting the dirt is not nearly as big a deal as God getting inside the hearts of the people we love.

LET'S GO TO WORK

"And when they had come to the multitude, a man came to Him, kneeling down to Him, saying, 'Lord, have mercy on my son, for he is an epileptic and suffers severely; for he often falls into the fire and often into the water. So I brought him to your disciples, but they could not cure him. Then Jesus answered and said, 'O faithless and perverse generation, how long shall I be with you? How long shall I bear with you? Bring him here to Me. And Jesus rebuked the demon, and it came out of him, and the child was cured from that very hour. Then the disciples came to Jesus privately and said, "Why could we not cast it out?" So Jesus said to them, Because of your unbelief; for assuredly, I say to you, if you have faith as a mustard seed, you will say to this mountain, 'Move from here to there,' and it will move; and nothing will be impossible for you. However, this kind does not go out except by prayer and fasting." (Matthew 17:14-21)

This boy lived in misery, and his father suffered as he watched his son struggle. This desperate father reached out to those who professed to know Jesus. They could not help the man or his son. This boy needed deliverance from the grip of the enemy, and Jesus taught them that kind of power only came from prayer and fasting.

"There's that 'F'word again, Pastor Bill."

Prayer and fasting work together. My mother fasted every Thursday, and I thought she was a religious nut! When God saved me, I discovered that fasting is found throughout the Bible. Peter fasted. John fasted. Paul fasted. More importantly, Jesus fasted, and He expected His church to follow His example. He said, "When you fast." (Matthew 6:16)

We live for more important things than food or entertainment. We are moved by the heart of God more than we are moved by the demands of our flesh, and we know that God loves people. God wants to deliver people. We need the power of the Holy Spirit because people all around us come with their desperate needs and their mountains. That kind of power comes from prayer and fasting. Our prayers matter. Our faith in God can move mountains. We can pray the prayers that bring healing and deliverance, the kind of prayers that can turn sinners from their errors and save them from death. We are His house of prayer. We show up with our hard hats and shovels in hand. It is time to pray!

"The effective, fervent prayer of a righteous man avails much." (James 5:16)

Chapter Eight

DIRECTIVE

TAG! YOU'RE IT!

TO BE CONTINUED

"For by grace you have been saved through faith, and that not of yourselves; it is the gift of God, not of works, lest anyone should boast. For we are His workmanship, created in Christ Jesus for good works, which God prepared beforehand that we should walk in them." (Ephesians 2:8-10)

People come up to me and ask, "How can I serve God?" or "How do I know what God wants me to do?"

I always answer their question with a question of my own. "Have you received the gift?"

What gift are you talking about, Pastor Bill?

I am talking about the gift of salvation. No one can earn enough merit badges to achieve the rank of "Child of God." We can do all the good deeds and spiritual rituals we want. We can try to observe all of the commandments, but we will always come up short. Despite our best efforts, our lives will always be fraught with a list of shouldas, couldas, and wouldas.

The good news is there was one who did it. He did all of it. He kept all the laws and the rules. He paid all of the fees and penalties, and He gives us the benefits for free. None of us deserves salvation. Salvation is a free gift, and the only catch to this "too good to be true" offer is that we have to receive it.

If people respond to my first question with "yes", I then ask them, "When did you receive the gift?"

If they cannot remember, chances are they never did, so I ask them, "Would you like to?

Most of the time, they do. We cannot do anything for the Kingdom until we receive the gift, but once we say "yes," then we are on the clock. We are not saved by our efforts, but we are saved for the good works that He has already prepared for us.

EQUIPPING THE SAINTS

"And He Himself gave some to be apostles, some prophets, some evangelists, and some pastors and teachers, for the equipping of the saints for the work of ministry, for the edifying of the body of Christ," (Ephesians 4:11-12)

We are already saints. We do not earn our way into sainthood. I remember the first time someone tagged me for ministry. I was seventeen years old, brand new in the Lord, and my youth pastor, Roger, took me with him on a door-to-door outreach. I felt honored that my youth pastor chose me for something so important!

Next, a girl named Sue, who married my youth pastor, chose me to go on a choir tour. I warned her, "I cannot sing," but she did not care. She tagged me.

My cousin, Ruth Ann, tagged me to come to Bible College. Jim Andrews tagged me and taught me how to preach. I did not think I could do any of that stuff until I realized that someone believed in me. They tagged me and equipped me. If they had not tagged me, I would have never preached my first sermon.

We do not engage our spiritual gifts just to have a grand ole time in church. Hear me! It is great when we come together like that, but our spiritual gift is not meant to be contained within the four walls of our building, nor is it meant to be used to impress each other.

The Holy Spirit empowers us to point to Jesus Christ. The Holy Spirit's ministry is to glorify Jesus. That is the purpose of the Church. That is the purpose of Grace Church. That is the purpose of Bill Gehm.

How can we serve God? We live to glorify Jesus Christ in everything we do and in every place we go. We lift up Jesus so that other people can get saved. We do everything according to the Word of God.

"And it came to pass, at the time of the offering of the evening sacrifice, that Elijah the prophet came near and said, 'LORD God of Abraham, Isaac, and Israel, let it be known this day that You are God in Israel and I am Your servant, and that I have done all these things according to Your word. Hear me, O LORD, hear me, that this people may know that You are the LORD God, and that You have turned their hearts back to You again." (I Kings 18:36)

Elijah did not draw Israel near so that they could be impressed by him. He did not call down fire to enthrall his audience with a spectacular show. He drew them near so that they could hear the Word of God. He lifted up the name of the Lord God. He called down the fire so that the people would turn their hearts back to God. It was never about him. It was about God and His people.

PERFECT GOD - IMPERFECT VESSELS

"But God has chosen the foolish things of the world to put to shame the wise, and God has chosen the weak things of the world to put to shame the things which are mighty;" (2 Corinthians 1:27)

Elijah's life was the stuff of legends! He was an iron man of God and a great prophet, but he was not perfect, and he did not have it all together. Do not forget about 1 Kings 19.

Elijah had a complex. He thought he was alone, and no one served God like him. So he said, "I have been very zealous for the LORD God of hosts;...I alone am left." (1 Kings 19:10)

That sounds a lot like pride and selfishness to me, Elijah. What about the widow who took a chance on you, sacrificed, and provided for you in the middle of a drought? What about Obadiah, who stayed behind while God took you away? Obadiah risked everything to hide 100 prophets in a cave. You are going to find out later, Elijah, that you were not the only one. 7000 people still stood strong and refused to bow to Baal.

Elijah thought his best days lay behind him. He might as well give up. It was enough!

"Now, LORD, take my life, for I am no better than my fathers!" (1 Kings 19:4)

This was not a prayer of surrender. This was a prayer of defeat. After all, he was a dead man anyway, right?

"And they seek to take my life." (1 Kings 19:10)

That sounds a lot like doubt and fear to me, Elijah. What about when God answered your prayers by shutting off the heavens? What about the three and a half years that God hid you away and provided for your every daily need? What about the fire and the rain? What about the defeat of 850 prophets of Baal against the one prophet of God? Do you really think God cannot handle the threat of one wicked and crazy queen? Do you really think God does not care about you?

He sounded just like us! That is because he was just like us, a man with a nature like ours. God uses us with our faults, our complexes, and our messes, and He does not throw us away when we struggle with selfishness, doubt, pride, or fear.

Are you burned out? Do you feel like you are getting too old? Do you feel like your past is too dark? Did you drop out? Guess what?! God does not care.

Repent! Drop back in! It is never too late. Fan the flame of the Holy Spirit, and allow Him to ignite your fire again. God used people of all backgrounds, including ex-murderers. God purposefully chooses the weak and base things so that He alone receives the glory. None of us can boast about our greatness, but we can all boast about our great God!

Pick up your cross, follow Jesus, and go to work.

THE WORK CONTINUES

God's solution to Elijah's fear and doubt was to stand him back up and put him back to work.

"Then the LORD said to him: Go, return on your way to the Wilderness of Damascus; and when you arrive, anoint Hazael as king over Syria. Also, you shall anoint Jehu, the son of Nimshi, as king over Israel. And Elisha, the son of Shaphat of Abel Meholah, you shall anoint as prophet in your place." (1 Kings 19:15-16)

God was not done with Elijah.

Maybe you feel like God is finished with you. You ran too far. You stayed away too long.

Maybe you think, "There's no way God would want me now."

Let me remind you, for we are His workmanship, created in Christ Jesus for good works, which God prepared beforehand that we should walk in them.

Hear me. God planned your works before we even knew who He was. He has not given up on Israel, and He has not given up on you. Now, today, is the time to stand up and go back to work.

God's solution to Elijah's loneliness and burnout was to give him a partner and protegee. We never find Elijah under the broom tree again after meeting Elisha. Elisha was more than just a companion and a partner. Elisha would be Elijah's replacement. Elijah tagged Elisha, and Elisha had to make a decision.

In 1 Kings 19:19, Elijah found Elisha plowing in the field and threw his mantle on him.

"And he left the oxen and ran after Elijah, and said, 'Please let me kiss my father and mother, and then I will follow you.... Then he arose and followed Elijah, and became his servant." (1 Kings 19:20-21)

In Bible College, Jim Andrews tagged me and taught me how to preach. Pastor Johnson was the father of Lucinda Joy Johnson, who would become Lucinda Joy Gehm. Gordon Schroeder tagged me to come to Amarillo in 1980.

I still have a pastor to whom I submit. His name is Rick Coburn, and he said, "Tag. you're it! You're going to Africa!" I decided fifty-two years ago to follow Jesus Christ, and I've had the privilege to tag others and watch them make the decision to follow Jesus and go to work. It is the only way to live.

SCALAWAGS OF YAHWEH

"Now, when the sons of the prophets who were from Jericho saw him, they said, 'The spirit of Elijah rests on Elisha.' And they came to meet him, and bowed to the ground before him. Then they said to him, "Look now, there are fifty strong men with your servants. Please let them go and search for your master, lest perhaps the Spirit of the LORD has taken him up and cast him upon some mountain or into some valley. And he said, "You shall not send anyone. But when they urged him till he was ashamed, he said, "Send them!" Therefore, they sent fifty men, and they searched for three days but did not find him. And when they came back to him, for he had stayed in Jericho, he said to them, 'Did I not say to you, "Do not go?" (2 Kings 2:15-18)

Elijah and Elisha's ministry created a holy jealousy, and the school of prophets wanted to be just like them. They were the scalawags of Yahweh. They watched the whirlwind carry Elijah away. They watched Elisha take up his mantle and part the Jordan. They wanted to serve God and be used by Him.

They wanted to experience a life beyond what they could have imagined. They were zealous and motivated. They begged to look for Elijah's body.

Maybe God carried him away to another mountain. Their hearts were in the right place, but they were immature and untrained. Elijah mentored Elisha, and now Elisha would train these prophets.

That is what we do in the Body of Christ. We look out for each other. We encourage each other. We mentor and strengthen each other.

Grace Church is a scalawag kind of church, founded by a bunch of kids who did not really understand what they were doing. We just knew that we wanted to be used by God in a real way. I was twenty-nine years old. My wife was pregnant with our third child. None of us was trained in church planting. We were young. We were inexperienced. We got the main thing right, but we got some things wrong.

Along the way, God guided us and matured us through His Word, and He sent people to guide us, encourage us, develop us, and mentor us. Many of us who started Grace Church now get to train up, encourage, and equip a whole host of volunteers who help make Grace Church possible. Our volunteer pool has grown so large that we ran out of parking spaces in our main parking lot for our volunteers and our church attendees. I had to ask them to park in an auxiliary parking lot adjacent to our main parking lot so that there would be enough parking spaces to make room for new people.

Did they fuss about the inconvenience or the extra steps they now have to take to get into the building? No! They want to serve God and be used by Him just like He used Elijah and Elisha, just like He used me and seventeen other people. He is still the same God, and the Kingdom of God is worth the extra effort to them.

TODAY IS THE DAY

Paul wrote, "One thing I do, forgetting those things which are behind and reaching forward to those things which are ahead, I press toward the goal for the prize of the upward call of God in Christ Jesus." (Philippians 3:13-14)

I have a great history with God, and I love to look back and remember, but I cannot get stuck there. We move forward, advancing the Kingdom of God, because there are still men and women who need to hear the Gospel. There are still men and women waiting to be saved. The fields are ready. The harvest is great, but the workers are few.

I do not know what the future has in store for me, but I know that following Jesus was, is, and will always be the best decision I made. I cannot imagine settling down and backing off now, not when I am so close to home. I refuse to spend the remainder of my days in a rocking chair on a porch somewhere.

Meet Toni Perriman, "Toni the Tiger". I did not give her that nickname. Someone else did. Forty-four years ago, her daughter was in my youth group. She was married to Gary Perriman, a pastor and evangelist in Amarillo. Hundreds came to Christ because of this couple. Years ago, Gary suffered a stroke that landed them in one of the retirement homes where I preached. God took Gary home, and "Toni the Tiger" was left behind. If anyone had an excuse to stop and stay under the broom tree, it was Toni, but she did not. She jumped in at Northwest Village and became the foundation for that Bible study. She found out she could also attend Bible study at Winwood Village on Thursdays. She sold a cemetery plot and donated the money to Grace Church. She joined our bus ministry. At seventy-three years old, she started riding our bus so she could love on the children that rode the bus to church. It never crossed her mind to stop.

She could have. She could have thought, "I already did a lot for the Kingdom of God, so I'm just going to wait it out until my time comes," but she did not! She kept moving forward, following Jesus all the way to glory, when God called her home after she had a stroke. She was a scalawag of Yahweh until the very end.

I say this in love. Church, it's time to grow up and go to work. I want you to know your spiritual gift. I do not want you to come into my church and hide out. I want to find you, tag you, and put you to work. Every part of the body is knitted together, and every part has to do its share. We need you.

Serving God is work. I do not fall asleep and allow God to just download sermons into my brain. I sit down with the Holy Spirit. I study the Scriptures, and together, we dig it out! It is work.

Part of my job is to get you ready to go to work.

I do not want to even think about what my life would have been like if Jesus had not saved me. I cannot think of a better way to live my life than to follow Jesus and do the works He has prepared for me.

It's been the greatest ride, and now I am tagging you. You are it!

Chapter Nine

DAY OF THE LORD

COMING HOME

MOUNTAIN EXPERIENCE

My family moved from Orlando, Florida, to Denver, Colorado, when I was twelve years old. My father took us camping up high in the Rocky Mountains. I will never forget the smell of the forest, the soothing rustle of the pine trees, or the sky so full of stars that it looked like someone sprinkled the sky with glitter. The next morning, snow began to fall. Orlando didn't have snow. It was beautiful, and I fell in love. I was made to be a mountain man. It was my first Rocky Mountain high, and I did not need to smoke anything to attain it.

Several years later, when Grace Church joined the Calvary Chapel fellowship, I attended a pastor's retreat just around the corner from where we went camping thirty years before. A different kind of beauty surrounded me as I met with pastors just like me, men who were in love with Jesus. I had a spiritual Rocky Mountain high.

I love mountain top experiences. We all do. That is a God-given desire that stems from our longing to be in God's presence and commune with Him, small glimpses of a greater mountain to come.

I often imagine traveling back in time to when Elijah actually walked on the earth, and I think about what I would say to the man who actually lived out the words I have read and the sermons I have preached.

1 Kings 18 is one of my favorite chapters in the entire Bible. In my mind, Mount Carmel has always defined Elijah's life and his ministry-the ultimate mountaintop experience with God. I think Elijah would agree with me that it was a glorious experience, but I do not think he would list Mount Carmel as his favorite mountain because Elijah would have another mountain top experience years and years after his time on earth was done.

THE MOUNT OF TRANSFIGURATION

"Now, after six days, Jesus took Peter, James, and John, his brother, led them up high on a mountain by themselves; and He was transfigured before them. His face shone like the sun, and His clothes became as white as light." (Matthew 17:1-2)

Jesus took three of His disciples, Peter, James, and John, on a mountain retreat. Guess who they saw on top of that mountain? Elijah, 800 years after Elijah departed for heaven. This was a close encounter of the right kind, but to understand the significance of the events on this mountain, we have to go back and pick up its context.

THE QUESTION

"When Jesus came into the region of Caesarea Philippi, He asked His disciples, saying, 'Who do men say that I, the Son of Man, am?" So they said, 'Some say John the Baptist, some Elijah, and others Jeremiah or one of the prophets. He said to them, "But who do you say that I am?" (Matthew 16:13-15)

Everywhere Jesus went, there was a crowd. He came up from His wilderness of testing and began preaching the Word of God. He sounded a lot like John the Baptist.

Jesus heard from God. He spoke with great confidence and authority as He revealed wisdom and insight into God's kingdom, including future events to come. He looked and sounded like the great prophets of Israel.

He performed mighty miracles. He was larger than life. He confronted corrupt religious leaders and called them out on their hypocrisy. He knew His message would incite vengeance, and they would try to kill Him, but He preached anyway. He looked and sounded a lot like Elijah.

Although no one could agree on who Jesus was, they all agreed He was someone special. But who? A great teacher? A wise man? Everyone had an answer, but not everyone had the right answer.

People are fickle. "We the people" does not always mean we're right. Everyone will have to answer that question, and we cannot look to the right or left to see what our neighbor says. We cannot call up our friends or family or even our minister to find out what their answer is.

We answer that question for ourselves. This is the most important test we will ever take, and it consists of only one question with only one right answer.

THE CORRECT ANSWER

"Simon Peter answered and said, "You are the Christ, the Son of the living God. 'Jesus answered and said to him, 'Blessed are you, Simon Bar-Jonah, for flesh and blood has not revealed this to you, but My Father who is in heaven." (Matthew 16:16-17)

Simon Peter had spouted off some crazy things over the past couple of years, but this time he got it right. He knew who Jesus was: The Christ, the Anointed One, the Son of the Living God. The devil cannot stand up against that truth, and he can't destroy the person who receives the revelation of who Jesus Christ is. All of the answers to all of life's questions are wrapped up in The One Answer, Jesus Christ.

The answer is simple, but that does not mean life gets easier when we know it. Peter knew the answer, but life was about to get more complicated.

THE CROSS IS COMING

"From that time, Jesus began to show His disciples that He must go to Jerusalem, and suffer many things from the elders and chief priests and scribes, and be killed, and be raised on the third day. Then Peter took Him aside and began to rebuke Him, saying, "Far be it from You, Lord; this shall not happen to You!" But He turned and said to Peter, 'Get behind Me, Satan! You are an offense to Me, for you are not mindful of the things of God, but the things of men." Then Jesus said to His disciples, "If anyone desires to come after Me, let him deny himself, and take up his cross, and follow Me. For whoever desires to save his life will lose it, but whoever loses his life for My sake will find it. For what profit is it to a man if he gains the whole world, and loses his own soul? Or what will a man give in exchange for his soul?" (Matthew 16:21-26)

The Jews held to a specific picture of what the Messiah would look like. The problem was that they viewed Him through the lens of human understanding. Jesus looked nothing like the warrior that Israel had envisioned. Instead of talking about praise and glory, Jesus talked about rejection and betrayal. Instead of talking about victory and conquest, Jesus talked about suffering and surrender.

Before Jesus could be the roaring Lion of Judah, He had to become the silent Lamb of God. Peter knew Jesus was the King, but Peter did not understand the chief principle that governed His kingdom: love.

God so LOVED the world. John 3:17 says that Jesus did not come to condemn the world, but to save the world through Himself.

That meant carrying a cross. Peter tried to talk Jesus out of going to the cross. That is devil talk, Peter! Anyone or anything that would try to stop the work of the cross would be trying to stop the work of God. Jesus set His face like flint toward Jerusalem, and He did not need the distraction of a man who did not understand the mind or the heart of God.

Jesus's death on the cross would be the greatest moment in history. If Peter wanted to follow Jesus, he would have to carry a cross too. So will we. Do not listen to anyone who says Christianity is the key to an easy life. Christianity is the key to eternal and abundant life, filled with mountains and valleys, filled with crosses and crowns.

Wait a minute, Pastor Bill. It is one thing for Jesus to bear the cross, but you are saying I gotta bear a cross too? I am not into crosses.

I am not into crosses either. The cross wants to kill me. The cross is the thing that crucifies our flesh. God knows the cross we bear, but we do not bear ours alone. He is with us, and His burden is light. If it ended there, we would all be depressed, but let me remind you that Jesus is not on the cross now. He is alive, and He is coming back again in all of His glory, and we will trade our crosses for crowns.

"For the Son of Man will come in the glory of His Father with His angels, and then He will reward each according to His works. Assuredly, I say to you, there are some standing here who shall not taste death till they see the Son of Man coming in His Kingdom." (Matthew 16:27-28)

THE BIG REVEAL

"Now, after six days, Jesus took Peter, James, and John, his brother, led them up on a high mountain by themselves; and He was transfigured before them. His face shone like the sun, and his clothes became as white as the light." (Matthew 17:1-2)

The Greek word used in verse two is *metamorhoo*, which means to change into another form from within. The Mount of Transfiguration revealed the true nature of Jesus Christ and the glory He carried inside Himself during His entire time on earth. He did not change into His holy nature like one who puts on His Sunday best. His human form concealed His glory like a cloak. The cloak was peeled back, and the fullness of Christ's glory became exposed. God dwells in unapproachable light (1 Timothy 6:16), which cannot now or ever be viewed with human eyes, but here on the mountain, they stood with the Light of the World, the Light about which the Apostle John would remember and write.

Jesus was not merely a prophet, or a teacher, or a healer, or some mystical figure. He was, is, and will always be Jesus Christ, Almighty God the Son. The miracle was not the big reveal. The miracle was that who He truly was would be hidden so that we could come near Him.

"And behold, Moses and Elijah appeared to them, talking with Him. Then Peter answered and said to Jesus, Lord, it is good for us to be here; if You wish, let us make here three tabernacles: one for You, one for Moses, and one for Elijah." (Matthew 17:3-4)

Moses and Elijah appeared, seemingly out of nowhere. The boundaries between heaven and earth, time and space, past, present, and future vanished in the presence of Jesus' glory, as they all stood with the Ancient of Days, who was, is, and is to come.

The Bible says we will know as we are known (1 Corinthians 13:12), and somehow the disciples knew, "This is Moses and Elijah." The stories were true. They really did exist. Peter became caught up in the emotion and the grandeur of the moment, and the desire to worship bubbled up. This desire was good. It was even holy, but Peter reacted before he understood, and he spoke before he listened.

Moses wrote the Law, which pointed to Jesus. Elijah was a great prophet, larger than life, but he was a shadow and a type that pointed to Jesus. They deserved respect, but not worship! It is all too easy for people to fix their gaze on man, particularly men and women who point to or lead them to Jesus Christ. Radio waves, TV stations, and internet sites are filled with men and women preaching the Word. We live in an era of the "celebrity preacher". Hear me. A minister of the Gospel deserves respect, but there is only One who deserves the glory, the worship, and the credit, and that is Jesus Christ. We point people to Jesus Christ. We direct all the praise, glory, and honor, and all the admiration, adulation, and adoration to Jesus Christ. He alone is worthy!

ONLY JESUS

"While he was still speaking, behold, a bright cloud overshadowed them; and suddenly a voice came out of the cloud, saying, 'This is My beloved Son, in whom I am well pleased. Hear Him!' And when the disciples heard it, they fell on their faces and were greatly afraid. But Jesus came and touched them and said, 'Arise, and do not be afraid. When they had lifted up their eyes, they saw no one but Jesus only." (Matthew 17:5-8)

God will not share His glory with another. Do not put Jesus in the same sentence as Moses and Elijah. They did not glow. They did not shine. They were men with a nature just like ours.

The glorious nature belonged to Jesus, and only to Jesus. When the disciples looked up, they saw only Jesus, the fulfillment of Moses's law and the embodiment of Israel's prophets. The voice of the Father terrified the disciples, and they fell on their faces, but Jesus came to them and touched them. Jesus removed their fear, and they could stand under the gaze of the Father because of Jesus, only Jesus.

When I crashed my motorcycle, on my way down that hill, all I could think about was, "Today, I meet my Maker. I'm going to stand in the presence of Almighty God," and I knew I did not have a prayer. Terror gripped my heart, but Jesus met me at the bottom of that hill. He touched my heart, and He became my prayer. "Jesus, save me! I surrender!" When I lifted my eyes and looked around, all I saw was Jesus, not my friend, not my bike, only Jesus.

Jesus became the mediator between God and man. Because He was God, the fullness of God's glory dwelt in Him. Through Him, we can stand in the presence of the Almighty God and cry, "Abba Father!" We will behold God the Father as He is, in all of His light and glory. Because we will be like Him. (1 John 3:2) Because of Jesus, only Jesus!

He was not like Elijah or Moses. He was better. He was the better covenant. He was, is, and will always be God.

Moses was the author of Genesis-how it all began. John was the author of Revelation -how it will all end. Both are bookends to the Bible, and at the center of it all is Jesus Christ, the Alpha and Omega, the First and the Last. Jesus, the author of salvation. The Author of it all.

DESTINY OF THE SAINTS

Shortly after Elijah came off Mount Carmel, he entered his valley of depression. I think he might have looked back to gaze upon that mountain, thinking that the best had come and gone. It is why he prayed for his life to end then and there. But Elijah did not yet know the full story, and neither do we. Our perception is limited by our human understanding. We live in a kingdom that surrounds us, but the veil of human nature obscures the view of what we can see, like a reflection in a darkened mirror.

Moses, Elijah, and Jesus discussed what was about to happen. "And behold, two men talked with Him, who were Moses and

Elijah, who appeared in glory and spoke of His decease which He was about to accomplish at Jerusalem." (Luke 9:30-31)

Moses was a man among men in the Kingdom of God, but he was just a man. Moses met the Great I AM at the burning bush. God dictated, and Moses transcribed the Law. He knew about the altar and the sacrifice. Jesus said, "I AM here to fulfill the Law. 1 AM the Altar. I AM the sacrifice." Jesus is the Great I AM.

Peter did not want Jesus to talk about death, suffering, or the cross, and he wanted to stay on the mountain forever. The Mount of Transfiguration looked like the perfect place to stake a claim and build the new Kingdom of God. All "the greats" were there: Peter, James, John, Moses, and Elijah. The Messiah was there, the King of kings, so why not?

Peter failed to understand that ultimate glory would come at the ultimate price of sacrifice. If he wanted to follow Jesus, he would have to come down from the mountain. When Jesus decided to leave the Mount of Transfiguration, He finalized His decision to embrace the suffering, the cross, and ultimately His death, for He understood that His temporary death would yield everlasting life, not for Him. He was already from everlasting to everlasting. His death would give us life. He understood that His suffering would bring Salvation. Not for Him. He was already the perfect Lamb, but His sacrifice brought us Salvation.

Peter later wrote, "Of this salvation the prophets have inquired and searched carefully, who prophesied of the grace that would come to you, searching what, or what manner of time, the Spirit of Christ who was in them was indicating when He testified beforehand the sufferings of Christ and the glories that would follow. To them it was revealed that, not to themselves, but to us they were ministering the things which now have been reported to you through those who have preached the gospel to you by the Holy Spirit sent from heaven-things which angels desire to look into." (1 Peter 1:10-12)

Elijah was a prophet among prophets. Whether he stood in the courts of kings or sat at the table with Gentiles, Elijah declared God's Word and spoke of what was to come. Everything about the ministry of the prophets pointed to Jesus. Jesus revealed, "I am the substance of what was once shadow and symbolism."

We can see by faith, like a reflection in a dimly lit mirror, but the day will come when we will see everything in perfect clarity, exactly as it is. (1 Corinthians 13:12)

God restored Elijah, and he continued to have a powerful ministry, but he laid it all down the minute God said, "Elijah, it's time to come home." If I could sit down and speak with Elijah today, I think he would love talking about his mountaintop experience with God on Mount Carmel, but I also think he would tell me that Mount Carmel was nothing compared to gazing upon the glory of the Son of God on the Mount of Transfiguration. It was all about Jesus. It has always been about Jesus.

Peter left the mountain, and he chose to follow Jesus all the way to his own death on his own cross. James followed Jesus to his death. He was the first disciple to be martyred for his faith. John followed Jesus all the way to exile and rejection on the Isle of Patmos. Why? Because they remembered this day. They knew the glory that awaited them after the suffering. They had a front row seat to the arrest and torture of Jesus Christ. They understood better than most the price that was paid for our atonement. They understood the wonder of grace better than most, for they saw the glory of the Son of God.

Elijah's life did not end with the whirlwind. It was just the beginning. The prophet Malachi predicted the return of Elijah before the great day of the coming of the Lord.

Jesus revealed to them that the moment had passed as John the Baptist came in the spirit of Elijah. Elijah beheld the glory of Jesus on the Mount of Transfiguration. James tags him in his letter about prayer. He shows up again in The Revelation. Elijah is coming back. Jesus is coming back. He will touch down on the Mount of Olives (Zechariah 14), and we will be with Him as part of the armies of heaven. I have had many mountaintop experiences on earth. God has been so good to me. Grace Church on "Mount Amarillo" has been my life's work. It defines my call and my purpose on earth.

My wife and my family are my heart, but when I hear the voice of my Savior say, "Come up here." I am going to lay it all down to go be with the Lord. Mount Zion is my destiny. Mount Zion is the City of God, and Jesus Christ is its cornerstone. Moses and Elijah will be there, along with Peter, James, and John. Bill Gehm will join them. My prayer is that you will join us as we look at Jesus Christ in all of His glory!

I think Elijah will lay Mount Carmel at the feet of Jesus and say, "It was all worth it." I think I will lay Grace Church at the feet of Jesus, and I will say, "It was all worth it." We will all yield our crowns, our trophies, and our glory to the Glory of Jesus Christ, who will be the Light of that Holy City. He is worth it!

The best part is that we will never have to leave the mountain. So shall we be forever with the Lord.

THE END

www.ingramcontent.com/pod-product-compliance
Lightning Source LLC
La Vergne TN
LVHW020714110826
845149LV00012B/2256

* 9 7 9 8 9 9 5 4 9 2 9 0 0 *